Chinese Menus

This edition published 1994 by Bloomsbury Books, an
imprint of The Godfrey Cave Group, 42 Bloomsbury Street,
London, WC1B 3QJ.

© 1994 Time-Life Books BV.

ISBN 1 85471 556 9

Printed and bound in Great Britain.

Chinese Menus

Jean Yeub
Menu 1
Stuffed Courgettes	8
Home-Style Bean Curd	
Rice	

Menu 2
Lemon Chicken	10
Stir-Fried Carrots	
Rice	

Menu 3
Emerald Soup	12
Poached Fish Fillets, West Lake Style	
Fresh Snow Peas/Rice	

Barbara Tropp
Menu 1
Spicy Beef with Scallions and Sweet Red Peppers	16
Warm Chinese Noodles with Sesame Oil	
Hot and Sour Hunan Carrots	

Menu 2
Hoisin-Explosion Shrimp	18
Home-Style Spicy Eggplant	
Spicy Cold Noodles with Sesame Sauce and Seeds	

Menu 3
Steamed Spicy Fish with Black Mushrooms	22
Temple Fried Rice	
Cold-Tossed Watercress with Sesame Seeds	

Audrey and Calvin Lee
Menu 1
Seafood Treasure Noodles	28
Shatung Chicken with Hot Hoisin Sauce	

Menu 2
Lion's Head	30
Stir-Fried Cauliflower and Sweet Peppers	
Rice	

Menu 3
Corn Soup	
Red-Cooked Duck	32
Asparagus Salad/Rice	

Nina Simonds
Menu 1
Drunken Mushrooms	38
Baked Fish Packages with Ham and Mushroom	
Stir-Fried Lettuce/Rice	

Menu 2
Spicy Braised Spareribs	40
Tossed Noodle Salad	
Stir-Fried Cucumbers with Peanut Sauce	

Menu 3
Barbecued Chicken Livers	42
Shredded Chicken in Lettuce Packages	
Rice	

Michael Tong
Menu 1
Sautéed Scallops	46
Pork with Barbecue Sauce	
Broccoli with Sugar Snap Peas/Rice	

Menu 2
Egg Drop Soup with Tomato	48
Orange Beef	
Stir-Fried Bok Choy/Rice	

Menu 3
Bean Curd Salad with Peanuts	50
Steamed Sea Bass with Black Bean Sauce	
Chicken, Szechwan Style/Rice	

Jeri Sipe
Menu 1
Sweet and Sour Cucumber Salad	54
Quick Barbecued Pork	
Fish Steaks with Hot Sauce/Rice	

Menu 2
Spicy Fried Calf's Liver	56
Mountain Snow White Chicken/Rice	

Menu 3
Vegetable Balls with Sweet and Sour Sauce	58
Spicy Lamb with Tree Ear Mushrooms	
Sautéed Shrimp with Cucumbers/Rice	

Bloomsbury Books
London

Jean Yeuh

Menu 1
(*left*)
Stuffed Courgettes
Home-Style Bean Curd
Rice

A native of Shangai, Jean Yueh learned to cook professionally in Hong Kong, and her three menus reflect this southern-eastern approach. She blends the cooking techniques of these two regions and applies them to the ingredients easily available in supermarkets. Like all good Chinese cooks, Jean Yueh emphasises the freshest possible ingredients, so the techniques she uses here retain natural colours and nutrients.

Menu 1, with meat-stuffed courgettes, and Menu 3, with poached fish and chicken and spinach soup, are typical dishes of the eastern region. Menu 2 features a Cantonese favorite – lemon chicken. Each meal has contrasting textures but harmonizing flavours.

Jean Yueh's meals are fun to prepare, and they will help you to develop your skills, since she demonstrates a spectrum of techniques: poaching, steaming, blanching, stir frying, and deep frying. In her classes and her cookbooks, she simplifies her classic Chinese recipes by using modern kitchen appliances, such as the food processor; though she never sacrifices taste and appearance for the sake of speed.

Note: All tablespoon measurements in these recipes are level tablespoons, unless otherwise stated.

In addition to its uses as a cooking tool, a Chinese bamboo steamer is also a handsome serving dish for this stuffed courgettes. Or you can use any attractive plate or platter, lined with lettuce leaves. If the meal is informal, bring the stir-fried bean curd to the table in the wok or sauté pan and serve the rice in small bowls.

Stuffed Courgettes
Home-Style Bean Curd
Rice

Stuffed courgettes is a home-style Shanghai summer dish. Although Shanghai and the whole eastern region are known for their long-simmered dishes, the region abounds, too, in fish and fresh produce, which chefs cook quickly. This courgettes stuffed with ground pork is light and delicious – first steamed, then glazed with a brown sauce. It is especially good served with a bean curd dish.

Bean curd, also called 'tofu,' is an economical and adaptable food that is a Chinese staple. Made from soy beans, tofu has many merits: it is full of protien and vitamins, and free of cholesterol. Served alone, tofu tastes bland, but readily absorbs flavours from accompanying sauces or other ingredients. Firm tofu, which this recipe calls for, holds its shape so that it can be cut up or stir-fried without disintegrating. Avoid using soft bean curd, which will not work in this particular recipe. This home-style bean curd dish acquires a golden brown crust while remaining tender and moist within. Hot spices are not typical of the eastern region, but if you like spicy food, use the hot dried pepper or crushed red pepper flakes that Jean Yueh lists as optional.

What to drink
These dishes present a range of delicate, fresh flavours best complemented by a simple, light wine. An Italian Pinot Grigio, a California Pinot Blanc, or a German wine from the Moselle are all good choices.

Start-to-Finish Steps
1 Follow rice recipe steps 1 and 2.
2 Chop scallion, mince ginger, and drain water chestnuts. Follow courgette recipe step 1.
3 Follow bean curd recipe steps 1 and 2. Preheat oven to 200°C (400°F or Mark 6).
4 Follow courgette recipe steps 2 through 8. While courgettes are steaming, slice fresh ginger and drained water chestnuts for bean curd recipe. Follow recipe steps 3 and 4.
5 When courgettes are cooked, keep warm in oven. Follow rice recipe step 3.
6 If glazing courgettes, follow courgette recipe step 9 and keep warm while cooking bean curd.
7 Wipe out wok. Follow bean curd recipe steps 5 through 7. Follow rice recipe step 4.
8 Remove courgettes from oven. Complete courgette recipe step 10 and serve with bean curd and rice.

Stuffed Courgettes

500 g (1 lb) lean minced pork, or boneless pork loin ground in food processor
1 scallion, finely chopped
1 teaspoon finely minced fresh ginger
5 large water chestnuts, drained and minced
1 tablespoon plus $^1/_2$ teaspoon cornstarch
1 tablespoon dry sherry
$1^1/_2$ tablespoons plus 2 teaspoons light soy sauce
1 teaspoon sugar
2 courgettes (about 5 cm (2 inches) in diameter and 625 g ($1^1/_4$) pounds total weight)
Fresh coriander or Italian parsley sprigs for garnish (optional)
Lettuce leaves for garnish (optional)

For glaze (optional):
Chinese Chicken Stock, if necessary
2 teaspoons light soy sauce
$^1/_2$ teaspoon cornstarch mixed with 1 teaspoon water

1 In large bowl, combine ground pork, scallion, ginger, water chestnuts, 1 tablespoon cornstarch, dry sherry, $1^1/_2$ tablespoons soy sauce, and sugar. Mix thoroughly.
2 Wash courgettes. Cut off both ends, then cut each courgette crosswise into 8 rounds about 1 inch thick.
3 Use paring knife, teaspoon, or melon ball cutter to scoop out small hollow from each courgette section. Do not cut all the way through and leave rim about 5 mm ($^1/_4$ inch) thick.
4 Bring $2^1/_2$ cm (1 inch) water to a boil in a heavy 30 cm (12 inch) skillet or, if using bamboo steamer, in wok.
5 Spoon portion of pork mixture into each courgette section, mounding slightly. With moistened fingers, smooth top of filling.
6 Arrange stuffed courgette in 25 cm (10 inch) glass pie plate or other heatproof rimmed dish at least $2^1/_2$ cm (1 inch) smaller in diameter than skillet or in bamboo steamer, if using.
7 Set plate of stuffed courgettes on trivet over boiling water in skillet. Or you may place stuffed courgettes in bamboo steamer set in wok with water just below level of steamer.
8 Steam over medium-high heat about 20 minutes,

or until meat is cooked and courgettes are still slightly crisp. Test by tasting. Cook longer if you prefer very soft courgettes. You may serve courgettes at this point, or transfer cooked courgettes to serving platter and keep warm in oven while you prepare glaze that follows.

9   Measure 60 ml (2 fl oz) liquid from plate on which courgettes were steamed. If necessary, add enough chicken stock to make 60 ml (2 fl oz). Place liquid in wok or small saucepan. Add 2 teaspoons soy sauce. Slowly stir cornstarch mixture into sauce. Heat to boiling, or until thin, translucent glaze is formed.

10 Pour sauce evenly over courgettes. Garnish with sprigs of coriander or Italian parsley, if desired. For serving in bamboo steamer, line tray with fresh lettuce leaves and arrange courgettes on top.

Home-Style Bean Curd

500 g (1 lb) fresh firm bean curd
1 medium-size green bell pepper
1 medium-size red bell pepper
175 ml (6 fl oz) Chinese Chicken Stock
2 tablespoons light soy sauce, or to taste
1 tablespoon dark soy sauce
1 tablespoon cornstarch
4 tablespoons corn, peanut, or vegetable oil
2 hot dried red peppers, or $1/2$ teaspoon dried red
    pepper flakes (optional)
2 scallions, cut in $2^1/2$ cm (1 inch) sections
5 water chestnuts, drained and sliced in 5 mm
    ($1/4$ inch) rounds
2 slices fresh ginger, about $2^1/2$ mm ($1/8$ inch) thick
1 tablespoon Oriental sesame oil (optional)

1   Drain bean curd in colander. If using 7.5 cm (3 inch) squares of bean curd, cut each piece into 4 equal triangles. If using vacuum-sealed 500 g (1 lb) block, cut into 4 equal pieces, then cut each piece into 2 equal triangles. Slice each triangle into half its thickness. There will be 16 triangles.

2   Blot bean curd triangles. Place on double of paper towels and press to absorb excess moisture.

3   Wash peppers and core. Remove seeds, halve, and cut peppers into $2^1/2$ cm (1 inch) strips, then into $2^1/2$ cm (1 inch) squares.

4   For sauce, stir to combine chicken stock, light and dark soy sauce, and cornstarch in medium-size bowl.

5   Heat wok or 25 cm (10 inch) skillet, then add cooking oil and heat on high until very hot. Fry bean curd and cook until both sides are golden

brown, about 5 minutes. Remove bean curd with slotted spoon and keep warm in preheated slow oven.

6   Reheat wok or skillet, adding more oil if less than 2 tablespoons remain. Add hot dried red peppers, if you are using them, or dried red pepper flakes, ginger, and scallions, and cook 30 seconds over medium heat. Discard hot peppers (not necessary if using red pepper flakes) and ginger. Add green and red bell peppers and water chestnuts. Stir-fry 1 to 2 minutes, then add bean curd.

7   Stir soy sauce mixture thoroughly and add to pan. Stir constantly over high heat until sauce has thickened. Add sesame oil if desired and stir to mix. Serve hot.

Rice

300 g (10 oz) long-grain rice
625 ml ($1^1/4$ pts) water

1   Wash rice by rubbing it between your hands in several changes of water to remove any excess starch.

2   Combine rice and water in $1^1/2$ ltr (3 pt) saucepan. Bring to a boil over high heat. Continue to boil rice, uncovered, about 5 minutes, until virtually all visible water has evaporated, leaving bubbles and air holes on surface of rice.

3   Cover pan and simmer over very low heat 18 or 20 minutes.

4   Uncover and stir well to fluff rice before serving.

Added touch

For an easy appetizer, toast shelled whole pecan pieces in a 180°C (350°F or Mark 4) oven 10 minutes, then cool to room temperature. Spread $1/4$ teaspoon *hoison* sauce or to taste over a small leaf of iceberg lettuce. Let each person wrap 2 to 3 pecan pieces in the lettuce leaf. For dessert, top lemon sherbet with coffee liqueur and sprinkle with grated lemon rind.

Lemon Chicken
Stir-Fried Carrots
Rice

Hong Kong, the culinary centre of the Orient, excels in the dishes of southern China, and one of the best of these is lemon chicken. The version here, with a cornstarch batter and a sauce flavoured with fresh lemon juice and soy, is light and easy to make. Some Hong Kong chefs use butter to enrich the sauce for this dish, though this is far from customary Chinese cooking. If you like a buttery sauce, follow their example and swirl in a tablespoon of unsalted butter as you finish making the sauce..

For additional flavour and colour, garnish the chicken with a combination of finely shredded lemon rind and carrot. Before juicing the lemons for the sauce, peel them lightly, without cutting into the white pith, and shred the strips.

To prepare the vegetables for stir frying, you need a very sharp knife, preferably a Chinese cleaver, to cut them precisely into neat matchstick-size pieces. The dish looks more attractive if the shreds are uniform, and the vegetables will cook through evenly. Because carrots are firm and require a slightly longer cooking time, you must stir-fry them before adding the courgette to the wok.

What to drink

A chilled dry white wine goes well with the lemon chicken. Try a Chardonnay (imported or domestic), which adapts to tart flavours. Beer or tea also good choices.

Start-to-Finish Steps

In the morning: Follow lemon chicken recipe steps 1 through 4.

1   Bring chicken to room temperature 30 minutes before cooking.
2   Follow rice recipe steps 1 and 2.
3   Preheat oven to 200°C (400°F or Mark 6).
4   Follow carrots and courgettes recipe, steps 1 through 4. If you wish to serve hot, turn into heatproof serving dish and place in oven. Otherwise, let sit at room temperature.
5   Follow rice recipe step 3.
6   Wipe out wok. Follow lemon chicken recipe steps 5 through 11.
7   Follow rice recipe step 4. Remove carrots and courgettes from oven and serve with lemon chicken and rice.

Crispy chicken breasts in lemon sauce with a stir fry or fresh vegetables make a delicate combination that you can serve on a single large platter. Light colours and clear glassware provide the right setting for this meal.

Lemon Chicken

3 whole skinless, boneless chicken breasts
1½ teaspoons of salt
¼ teaspoon freshly ground black pepper
¾ teaspoon sugar
2 teaspoons dry sherry
2 teaspoons light soy sauce
3 egg whites
125 g (4 oz) plus 1 tablespoon cornstarch
1 ltr (1¾ pts) corn, peanut, or vegetable oil
4 large leaves iceberg lettuce, washed and dried

Lemon sauce:
100 ml (3 fl oz) freshly squeezed lemon juice
1 tablespoon light soy sauce
¼ teaspoon salt, or to taste
5 tablespoons sugar, or to taste
4 teaspoons cornstarch
250 ml (8 fl oz) water

1 tablespoon corn, peanut, or vegetable oil
1 scallion, white part only, finely minced
1 tablespoon butter (optional)
2 lemons, sliced, plus shredded rind of additional
lemon for garnish (optional)

1   Cut each breast into halves. Detach small fillet underneath each half: you should have 2 large and 2 small pieces from each breast. Cut large pieces into halves.
2   In medium-size bowl, mix chicken thoroughly with salt, pepper, sugar, sherry, and soy sauce.
3   Beat egg whites until frothy. Put the 125 g (4 oz) cornstarch in another medium-size bowl. Dip the chicken, one piece at a time, into cornstarch, then into egg whites, then back into cornstarch until each piece is well coated.
4   Sprinkle the tablespoon of cornstarch on baking sheet. Place coated chicken in one layer on pan and refrigerate. (This can be done far in advance if time allows.)
5   Wash bowl in which chicken was marinated for sauce.
6   Heat 1 ltr (1¾ pts) cooking oil to 190°C (375°F) on deep-fat thermometer in wok or 3½ ltrs (6 pts) saucepan.
7   If desired, finely shred lettuce leaves and spread evenly on serving platter.
8   Combine sauce ingredients in medium-size bowl.
9   When oil is hot, fry chicken a few pieces at a time, until coating is set and chicken is cooked, 3 to 5 minutes. Remove with Chinese mesh or slotted metal spoon to drain on plate lined with paper towels. For crisper chicken, fry it twice, but do not fully cook the first time. Keep chicken warm in preheated slow oven.

10 Heat the 1 tablespoon of oil in a small saucepan. Add finely minced scallion and cook 30 seconds. Stir lemon sauce mixture thoroughly to recombine the corn starch and add to saucepan. Stir constantly until sauce is thickened and flows easily off spoon. Add butter if desired, and stir to combine.
11 Cut chicken into 1 cm (¾ inch) strips and arrange neatly on top of the shredded lettuce. Drizzle half of lemon sauce over chicken. Pour remaining sauce into bowl and serve with chicken. If desired, garnish with thinly sliced lemon and shredded lemon rind.

Stir-Fried Carrots and Courgettes

500 g (1 lb) courgettes
350 g (12 oz) carrots
3 tablespoons corn, peanut, or vegetable oil
¾ teaspoon salt, or to taste
½ teaspoon sugar

1   Wash courgettes and trim off both ends. Cut courgettes diagonally into 5 mm (¼ inch) thick and 5 cm (2 inch) long oval slices. Stack a few slices and cut 5 mm (¼ inch) shreds.
2   Peel carrots and cut similarly into 5 mm (¼ inch) shreds.
3   Heat wok or skillet until a bead of water immediately evaporates. Add oil and heat about 30 seconds, or until a carrot shred sizzles. Add carrots and stir-fry to coat with oil. Cover and cook 2 to 3 minutes, stirring 2 or 3 times.
4   Add courgettes, salt, and sugar. Stir-fry uncovered another minute, or until heated through. Serve hot or at room temperature.

Rice

300 g (10 oz) long-grain rice
625 ml (1¼ pts) water

1   Wash rice by rubbing it between your hands in several changes of water to remove any excess starch.
2   Combine rice and water in 1½ ltr (3 pt) saucepan. Bring to a boil over high heat. Continue to boil rice, uncovered, about 5 minutes, until virtually all visible water has evaporated, leaving bubbles and air holes on surface of rice.
3   Cover pan and simmer over very low heat 18 or 20 minutes.
4   Uncover and stir well to fluff rice before serving.

Emerald Soup
Poached Fish Fillets, West Lake Style
Fresh Snow Pea Salad / Rice

Fish fillets, snow pea salad, rice, and soup provide a meal that is simple enough for children to enjoy yet elegant enough for guests

West Lake poached fish is a speciality of Hangzhou, a lake resort in eastern China. The chefs there use only fresh-caught local fish, killed moments before cooking.

The gentle poaching technique used in this recipe retains the flavour and emphasizes the natural sweetness of fresh fish. You will achieve best results by using very fresh fillets of flounder or sole and not over cooking them.

Try to find a genuine Chinese red vinegar for making the sauce. Chinese rice-based vinegars are lighter and faintly sweeter than western ones. If you must substitute red wine vinegar, use a good grade and taste the sauce to see whether you need to add a touch more sugar.

What to drink
With this family-style dinner serve a light red wine such as a Beaujolais or a California Gamay or; if you prefer white, California Chardonnay or a French Mâcon or Graves.

Start-to-Finish Steps
1 Follow rice recipe steps 1 and 2.
2 Bring water to a boil for soup recipe and poached fish recipe, each step 1.
3 Shred scallion, if using, slice fresh ginger, and lightly crush and peel garlic cloves for poached fish.
4 Follow soup recipe steps 2 through 4.
5 Follow poached fish recipe steps 2 through 4.
6 Follow soup recipe steps 5 through 7. Preheat oven to 200°C (400°F or Mark 6).
7 Follow rice recipe step 3 and poached fish recipe step 5. Keep fish warm in oven.
8 Complete soup, steps 8 through 10, and keep warm.
9 Follow snow pea recipe steps 1 through 3.
10 Follow poached fish recipe step 8.
11 Follow snow pea recipe steps 4 and 5, and poached fish recipe step 9. Serve with rice.

Emerald Soup

125 g (4 oz) fresh spinach
1/2 skinless, boneless chicken breast
1 tablespoon plus 1 1/2 teaspoons cornstarch
1 teaspoon dry sherry
875 ml (1 2/3 pts) Chinese Chicken Stock
1 large egg white
2 tablespoons water
Salt
Freshly ground white pepper (optional)

1 Bring 1 ltr (1 3/4 pts) water to a boil in a large heavy saucepan.
2 Wash spinach well in several changes of water until no sand remains. Drain in colander.
3 Add spinach to the boiling water and bring water back to a boil, uncovered. Boil 30 seconds and quickly drain spinach in colander. Rinse under cold

running water.

4 Squeeze spinach to remove excess water and shred finely with cleaver or knife.

5 Cut chicken into $2^1/_2$ cm (1 inch) cubes. Place cubes in blender or food processor and add $1^1/_2$ teaspoons cornstarch, sherry, 60 ml (2 fl oz) chicken stock, and egg white. Blend until chicken is puréed. If using food processor, purée chicken cubes before adding remaining ingredients, then process just until well blended. Transfer mixture to bowl.

6 Combine remaining cornstarch and water in small bowl.

7 Bring the chicken stock to a boil in the saucepan used for the spinach.

8 Stir in puréed chicken mixture over low heat until it is well dispersed and chicken turns white.

9 Stir cornstarch mixture thoroughly and slowly add it to the hot soup, stirring constantly to prevent lumping. Bring soup back to a boil and cook 30 seconds.

10 Add chopped spinach and season with salt and white pepper. Keep warm, uncovered, in oven. Serve in soup tureen or in individual bowls.

Poached Fish Fillets, West Lake Style

4 very fresh fillets of flounder or sole (about 250 g (8 oz) each)
2 scallions, cut in half lengthwise
Four $2^1/_2$ mm ($^1/_8$ inch) slices fresh ginger plus 1 tablespoon minced
3 tablespoons dry sherry
2 medium-size cloves garlic, peeled and lightly crushed
3 tablespoons light soy sauce
4 tablespoons Chinese red rice vinegar, or 3 tablespoons Western red wine vinegar
3 tablespoons sugar, or to taste
175 ml (6 fl oz) Chinese Chicken Stock
4 teaspoons cornstarch mixed with 2 tablespoons water
2 tablespoons corn, peanut, or vegetable oil
1 tablespoon sesame oil (optional)
1 small scallion, cut into 5 cm (2 inch) lengths and finely shredded for garnish (optional)

1 In Dutch oven, bring $3^1/_2$ ltrs (6 pts) water to a boil. Wipe fish with damp paper towels.

2 Add scallions, sliced ginger, and 2 tablespoons sherry to boiling water. Combine garlic and minced ginger for sauce in small bowl or cup.

3 In another bowl, combine remaining sherry, soy sauce, vinegar, sugar, and chicken stock.

4 Stir to dissolve cornstarch and water in a small bowl.

5 When liquid returns to a boil, add fish. Cover and remove heat. Fillets should be done in 1 to $1^1/_2$ minutes, depending on their thickness. When transparency disappears, test to see if fish flakes easily. Gently lift fillets out, one at a time, with wide slotted spatula. Drain well and arrange over serving platter.

6 In a wok or small saucepan, heat the 2 tablespoons of cooking oil over medium heat. Add garlic and ginger, and fry 30 seconds. Discard garlic.

7 Add sherry-soy sauce mixture and bring to a boil over high heat.

8 Stir cornstarch mixture thoroughly and slowly add it to the sauce, stirring constantly to prevent lumping. Bring to a boil and simmer 30 seconds. Remove from heat and add sesame oil, if desired. Set aside.

9 Remove fish fillets from oven and pour off any liquid that may have accumulated around them. Pour sauce over fish and decorate with shredded scallion, if desired.

Fresh Snow Pea Salad

250 g (8 oz) fresh snow peas
125 g (4 oz) canned water chestnuts, drained
$1^1/_2$ tablespoons light soy sauce
1 tablespoon sesame oil

1 Bring $1^1/_4$ ltrs (2 pts) water to a boil in large heavy saucepan.

2 Pinch off stem ends of snow peas and pull off strings.

3 Cut water chestnuts into 5 mm ($^1/_4$ inch) round slices.

4 Add snow peas to the boiling water and cook 30 to 60 seconds. Quickly drain in colander and rinse under cold running water. Drain well and blot dry with paper towels.

5 Place snow peas and water chestnuts in serving bowl. Toss with soy sauce and sesame oil. Serve.

Rice

300 g (10 oz) long-grain rice
625 ml ($1^1/_4$ pts) water

1 Wash rice by rubbing it between your hands in several changes of water to remove any excess starch.

2 Combine rice and water in $1^1/_2$ ltr (3 pt) saucepan. Bring to a boil over high heat. Continue to boil rice, uncovered, about 5 minutes, until virtually all visible water has evaporated, leaving bubbles and air holes on surface of rice.

3 Cover pan and simmer over very low heat 18 or 20 minutes.

4 Uncover and stir well to fluff rice before serving.

Barbara Tropp

Menu 1
(*right*)
Spicy Hunan Beef with Scallions
and Sweet Red Peppers
Warm Chinese Noodles with Sesame Oil
Hot and Sour Hunan Carrots

As you sample an authentic Chinese meal, you will become aware of the delicate balance between one flavour and another, one texture and another. This balance derives from the Chinese philosophy of the duality of life – the *yin* and the *yang*, complementary opposites of human life, such as male and female, passive and active, sweet and sour. Barbara Tropp, a China scholar turned Chinese cook, brings this classic Chinese view of harmony to her cooking.

A native of New Jersey, Barbara Tropp spent two years in Taiwan, where she learned about Chinese food. After she returned to America, she became so homesick for Chinese cooking that she taught herself how to prepare Chinese meals. She has learned to adapt Chinese techniques to the fresh ingredients available in Western markets. Knowing that for most cooks speed is essential, she has revamped some of the lengthier traditional recipes to suite the often hectic pace of American life. She believes in practicality and economy – good taste above fancy presentation – so her menus do not require a large supply of extensive tools or ingredients.

Barbara Tropp favours the robust dishes of North China and the spicy hot foods of Szechwan and Hunan in the West. Menu 1 combines noodles with spicy beef – a popular northern dish – and hot and sour Hunan carrots. Menu 2, starring shrimp and eggplant, is a spicy Hunanese blend of chili, ginger, garlic, and scallions, and Menu 3 is multiregional.

Patterned china sets off this brilliant dinner, ideal for a winter evening. Add a sprig of parsley to the platter of hot and sour carrots and top the noodles with sesame seeds if desired. The right beef dish needs no garnish.

15

Spicy Hunan Beef with Scallions and Sweet Red Peppers
Warm Chinese Noodles with Sesame Oil
Hot and Sour Hunan Carrots

Both the beef and the noodle recipes call for a common Chinese ingredient – sesame oil. This dark brown nutty oil – a pantry basic – is not for cooking but for seasoning. Buy only a Chinese or Japanese brand; the cold-pressed health or Middle Eastern types will not do.

In the hot and sour Hunan carrots, red chilies will provide the hot taste, vinegar the sour, while the sprinkling of sugar enhances the flavour without sweetening the dish.

For this menu, the first step is to marinate the beef in the morning. At cooking time, you use a common Chinese technique that 'double cooks' an ingredient. You sear the beef quickly in hot oil, then stir-fry the other ingredients. For the last few seconds of cooking, you return the beef strips to the pan and combine all the ingredients.

What to drink
This spicy menu calls for a light, fruity wine with a touch of sweetness, such as a California Zinfandel.

Start-to-Finish Steps

In the morning: Follow Hunan beef recipe steps 1 and 2.

1 Follow warm Chinese noodles recipe step 1. While water comes to a boil, follow Hunan beef recipe steps 3 through 5.
2 Prepare carrots for Hunan carrots recipe step 1.
3 Wipe out wok. Follow Hunan beef recipe step 6.
4 Follow Hunan carrots recipe steps 2 through 4.
5 Follow Hunan beef recipe steps 7 through 12.
6 Follow Hunan carrots recipe steps 5 through 7.
7 Follow warm Chinese noodles recipe steps 2 and 3.

8 Follow Hunan carrots recipe step 8 and noodles recipe steps 4 through 6.
9 Remove beef and carrots from oven, and serve with warm noodles.

Spicy Hunan Beef with Scallions and Sweet Red Peppers

500 g (1 lb) round or flank steak, trimmed of fat and gristle

The marinade:
2 tablespoons light soy sauce
4 teaspoons cornstarch
1 teaspoon sugar
1 tablespoon corn or peanut oil

The sauce:
3 tablespoons Chinese rice wine or dry sherry
2 tablespoons light soy sauce
2 tablespoons sugar
1^1/$_2$ tablespoons *hoison* sauce
^{3}/$_4$ teaspoon sesame oil
8 whole scallions
1 red bell pepper, cored, seedes, and cut into thin strips
2 to 3 teaspoons finely minced garlic (about 3 cloves)
2 to 3 teaspoons finely minced fresh ginger
^{1}/$_2$ to ^{3}/$_4$ teaspoon dried red pepper flakes
750 ml–1 ltr (1^1/$_2$-2 pts) corn or peanut oil
^{1}/$_8$ teaspoon coarse salt
^{1}/$_8$ teaspoon sugar

1 Prepare beef and marinade. Holding cleaver or knife at angle, cut beef against grain into long strips about 2^1/$_2$ mm (^{1}/$_8$ inch) thick and 1 cm (^{1}/$_2$ inch) wide. Cut strips crosswise into 5 cm (2 inch) lengths.
2 Using fork, blend marinade ingredients in large bowl until smooth.
3 In a small bowl stir to combine sauce ingredients.
4 Trim wilted tops and root ends from scallions. Cut on sharp diagonal into thin ovals about 2^1/$_2$ cm (1 inch) long.
5 Core and seed pepper. Cut lengthwise into thinnest possible strips.
6 Combine garlic, ginger, and dried red pepper flakes in another small bowl.
7 Heat wok or Dutch oven high heat until hot

16

enough to evaporate a bead of water on contact. Add oil and heat to 180°C (350°F) on deep-fat thermometer, or until a slice of beef bubbles very slowly when added. While oil is heating, drain beef in metal colander nested in large bowl.

8 Stir beef once more, then gently slide slices into the oil. Carefully stir to separate beef slices and fry 15 seconds, just until beef is slightly grey.

9 Using pot holders, immediately pour beef and hot oil into metal colander. Or, working very fast you may use a Chinese mesh spoon or long-handled metal slotted spoon to scoop out the beef, then drain on paper towels. Turn off heat and allow oil to cool before pouring it off. Reserve.

10 Wipe out wok, leaving thin film of oil. Heat wok or heavy skillet over high heat until bead of water sizzles on contact.
Add 2 tablespoons of the hot oil and swirl it to coat pan. Reduce heat to medium. Add garlic, ginger, and pepper flakes, and stir about 10 seconds, adjusting heat so they do not brown.

11 Add red pepper strips and stir briskly to glaze them. Sprinkle with salt and sugar, then toss to combine, about 10 seconds in all. Drizzle in a bit more oil, if necessary, to prevent sticking. Lower heat if peppers begin to scorch.

12 Stir sauce mixture, then add to pan, stirring to combine. Raise heat slightly to bring mixture to bubbling point. Add beef and toss briskly to coat with sauce, about 5 seconds. Add scallions and toss briskly to coat with sauce, about 5 seconds. Do not let scallions wilt. Place in serving dish and keep warm in preheated slow oven.

Warm Chinese Noodles with Sesame Oil

500 g (1 lb) 1mm ($1/_{16}$ inch) thin Chinese egg noodles, fresh or dried
2 teaspoons coarse salt
2 tablespoons sesame oil
Fresh coriander or Italian parsley for garnish (optional)

1 Bring $4^{1}/_{2}$ ltrs (8 pts) unsalted water to a rolling boil in stock-pot or kettle.

2 If using fresh noodles, fluff them and add to the pot.

3 Using chopsticks or 2 long-handled wooden spoons, swish noodles gently back and forth several times to separate strands. Cook until a single strand tastes cooked but still firm to the bite.

4 Drain immediately in metal colander.

5 Return drained noodles to pot, combine with salt and sesame oil, toss well to coat each strand.

6 Turn onto heated serving platter and garnish with fresh coriander or Italian parsley sprigs, if desired. Serve.

Hot and Sour Hunan Carrots

750 g ($1^{1}/_{2}$ lb) baby carrots
$1^{1}/_{2}$ tablespoons salted black beans, coarsely chopped
$2^{1}/_{2}$ teaspoons finely minced garlic (about 2 cloves)
$2^{1}/_{2}$ teaspoons finely minced fresh ginger
$1/_{2}$ teaspoon dried red pepper flakes

The sauce:
125 ml (4 fl oz) unsalted Chinese Chicken Stock
2 tablespoons light soy sauce
$1^{1}/_{2}$ tablespoons unseasoned Oriental rice vinegar
$1/_{4}$ teaspoon sugar
$2^{1}/_{2}$ teaspoons cornstarch
$1^{1}/_{2}$ tablespoons Chinese Chicken Stock
$2^{1}/_{2}$ tablespoons corn or peanut oil

1 Peel and roll cut carrots.

2 Combine black beans, garlic, ginger, and red pepper flakes in saucer.

3 Combine sauce ingredients in small bowl, stirring to dissolve sugar.

4 Blend cornstarch and broth until smooth. Set aside.

5 Heat wok or heavy skillet over high heat until hot enough to evaporate a bead of water on contact. Add oil, swirling to coat pan, then reduce heat to medium-high. Add black bean mixture and stir gently until fully fragrant, about 10 seconds.

6 Add carrots and toss briskly to combine and glaze each nugget with oil, drizzling in a bit more oil from side of pan, if neccesary, to prevent sticking. Continue to toss until carrots feel hot to the touch, about 1 minute.

7 Stir sauce, then add to pan. Toss to combine it with the carrots, then raise the heat to bring liquids to a simmer. Level the carrots, adjust heat to maintain a steady simmer, then cover pan. Cook 3 to 4 minutes, until carrots are tender-crisp and still a bit underdone. Taste sauce and adjust with an extra splash of vinegar or a dash of sugar.

8 Stir cornstarch and chicken broth mixture quickly to recombine, then add to pan. Stir until glossy and slightly thick, about 10 seconds. Remove to heated serving bowl and keep warm in preheated slow oven.

<table>
<tr>
<td>

Menu

2

</td>
<td>

Hoisin-Explosion Shrimp
Home-Style Spicy Eggplant
Spicy Cold Noodles with Sesame Sauce and Seeds

</td>
</tr>
</table>

Hoisin-explosion shrimp are fresh shrimp cooked in the shell with *hoisin* sauce and wine. The 'explosion' comes during the stir fry, when the alcohol evaporates and the sauce bubbles on contact with hot metal, causing the fragrances and flavours of the shellfish, spices, and wine to their peak. This is a home-style meal, spicy but well-balanced in taste. The combination of shrimp and eggplant, soy sauce and vinegar, garlic and scallion unifies the meal and gives it a Hunanese character.

Most shrimp marketed today as fresh have been previously frozen and then thawed out in the fish market, but if you can buy truly fresh shrimp from a reliable fish store, do so. Otherwise look for a firm flesh, an intact shell, and a clean smell. The colour of the shell is not an indication of freshness; it varies depending on locality and may be grey or pink.

Cooking shrimp in the shell is a favourite Chinese method because the shell protects the tender shrimp and keeps it from drying out. Berore you cook the

Though both the shrimp and eggplant are peppery to the taste, they provide pleasing contrasts in texture and colour, which you can carry out in your table setting.

18

shrimp, devein it, being careful not to detach the shell. You and your guests will find it easy to shell the shrimp once the shell has been cut.

Oriental eggplants – either Japanese or Chinese – are smaller and sweeter than the Western ones, and their skins are edible. If these varieties are not available, choose small Western eggplants with smooth, unblemished skins; do not peel them.

The spicy cold noodles, tossed with the piquant sesame sauce and garnished with toasted sesame seeds, are especially good tasting and fun to eat. Fresh Chinese egg noodles are delicious, but if they are not available, select an Italian or Spanish dried egg noodle rather than a Chinese dried noodle.

Chinese black vinegar – used here to season the eggplant – is difficult to find. The best brand, according to Barbara Tropp, is Narcissus. Two readily available substitutes are Italian balsamic vinegar or California barengo vinegar, which you should be able to buy in any speciality food store.

Fresh coriander has a very pungent smell, unpleasant to some people, delightful to others. If you or your family and guests do not care for it, omit it and use Italian parsley instead.

What to drink

Chilled white is the appropriate drink to accompany this menu. Choose a California Sauvignon Blanc or Fumé Blanc for roundness and relative fullness. The cook also recommends a full-flavoured Gewürztraminer from California or, if you prefer, Japanese beer.

Start-to-Finish Steps

1 Follow spicy cold noodles recipe step 1 and set aside.
2 Follow eggplant recipe step 1.
3 Follow shrimp recipe steps 1 and 2.
4 Trim scallions for shrimp recipe step 3; trim and slice scallions for eggplant recipe step 2.

5 Follow spicy cold noodles recipe steps 2 and 3.
6 Follow eggplant recipe steps 3 and 4.
7 Follow cold noodles recipe steps 4 through 8.
8 Follow eggplant recipe steps 5 through 8 and shrimp recipe step 4.
9 Wipe out wok. Complete shrimp, steps 5 through 8.
10 Complete eggplant recipe step 9 and cold noodles recipe step 9, and serve with shrimp.

Hoisin-Explosion Shrimp

750 g (1¹/₂ lb) large fresh shrimp in the shell (15 to 20 shrimp)
2 scallions
1 tablespoon finely minced garlic (about 3 cloves)
¹/₂ to ³/₄ teaspoon dried red pepper flakes (optional)

The sauce:
2 tablespoons sugar
2 tablespoons *hoisin* sauce
2 tablespoons Chinese rice wine or dry sherry
2 tablespoons light soy sauce
¹/₂ teaspoon sesame oil
5 to 6 tablespoons corn or peanut oil
Fresh coriander sprigs for garnish (optional)

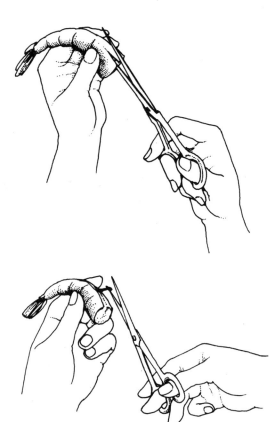

1 Using your fingers, pinch off legs of shrimp, several at a time, then bend back and snap of sharp, beaklike piece shell just above tail. Using scissors with straight, thin blades, cut through shell along back of each shrimp all the way to the tail, taking care to expose black digestive vein. Extract black vein with point of scissors. Be careful not to loosen shell.
2 Put shrimp in colander, rinse briefly with cool water, then dry with paper towels. Remove to medium-sized bowl and set aside.
3 Trim wilted green tops and roots from scallions. Cut scallions in half crosswise. Firmly grasp the pieces together and cut crosswise into 2¹/₂ mm (¹/₈ inch) rings. Put aside ¹/₂ tablespoon for garnish if you are not using coriander. Put remaining scallion rings, garlic, and red pepper flakes aside by side on small plate.
4 Stir to combine sauce ingredients in small bowl.
5 Heat wok or large heavy skillet over high heat until hot enough to evaporate a bead of water on contact. Add 5 tablespoons cooking oil, swirling to coat pan, then reduce heat to medium-high. Add garlic and stir so that it foams without browning. Add red pepper flakes and stir to combine. Then add scallion rings, again tossing several times to combine.
6 Add shrimp. Toss briskly 1 to 1¹/₂ minutes, until shrimp turn pink and shells are evenly glazed with oil. Adjust heat so shrimp sizzle without scorching. Drizzle in more oil, if necessary, to keep shrimp and seasoning from sticking.
7 Stir sauce briefly to recombine, then add to pan. Raise heat to 'explode' its fragrance (it will hiss and smell invitingly of wine), then toss briskly to combine. Toss until shrimp are evenly coated and sauce is slightly thick, about 10 seconds, then turn off heat.
8 Immediately transfer mixture to heated serving platter. Garnish with fresh coriander, if desired, or the reserved scallion rings.

Home-Style Spicy Eggplant

1 Kg (2 lb) firm, young firm eggplant, preferably long slender Oriental or small Italian variety
2 scallions
5 to 6 teaspoons finely minced garlic (about 5 to 7 cloves)
4 teaspoons finely minced fresh ginger
¹/₂ teaspoon dried red pepper flakes

The sauce:
200 ml (6¹/₂ fl oz) water
3 tablespoons light soy sauce

2 tablespoons plus 1 teaspoon brown sugar
2 teaspoons Chinese black or balsamic vinegar
125 ml (4 fl oz) corn or peanut oil
Dash black or balsamic vinegar
3/4 teaspoon Oriental sesame oil

1 Trim stem ends and brown base of eggplant, then roll cut. If using western eggplant, cut into pieces about 3 cm (1¼ inches) long, 2½ cm (1 inch) wide, and 2½ cm (1 inch) thick. Put in medium-size bowl and set aside.
2 Trim wilted green tops and roots from scallions and cut scallions crosswise in half. Firmly grasp the pieces together and cut them crosswise into 5 mm (¼ inch) rings. Reserve 2 teaspoons green and white rings for garnish.
3   Put remaining scallion rings, garlic, ginger, and pepper flakes side by side on small plate.
4 Stir to combine sauce ingredients.
5 Heat wok or large heavy skillet over high heat until hot enough to evaporate a bead of water on contact. Add cooking oil, swirling to coat pan, then reduce heat to medium-high. Add scallion rings,

garlic, and ginger. Stir to disperse them in the oil, adjusting heat so mixture foams without browning. Add pepper flakes. Stir gently about 10 seconds.
6 Add eggplant, tossing pieces to glaze them and pressing them gently against side of pan to encourage browning. Adjust heat so eggplant sizzles gently without scorching. As pan becomes dry, drizzle in another tablespoon of oil from the side. Continue tossing eggplant and pressing it against pan 3 to 4 minutes, until eggplant is brown-edged and a bit soft.
7 Briefly stir sauce ingredients and add them to pan. Toss gently to combine, then raise heat to bring liquids to a simmer. Cover tightly and adjust heat to bring liquids to a simmer. Cover tightly and adjust heat to maintain a lively simmer. Cook about 3 minutes, until liquids are absorbed, shaking pan to prevent eggplant from sticking.
8 Remove cover and toss eggplant. Add dash vinegar, sprinkle with sesame oil, then toss to combine.
9 Turn into serving dish, cover, and keep warm. Serve garnished with a sprinkling of the reserved scallion rings.

Spicy Cold Noodles with Sesame Sauce and Toasted Sesame Seeds

The sauce:
6 tablespoons sesame paste, drained of oil
5 tablespoons sesame oil
3 tablespoons light soy sauce
2 tablespoons sesame chili oil
2 tablespoons unseasoned Oriental rice vinegar
1 tablespoon plus 2 teaspoons sugar
2 to 3 tablespoons finely chopped fresh coriander
    leaves and upper stems (optional)
4 tablespoons water, approximately
2 tablespoons sesame seeds
350 g (12 oz) 1mm (1/16 inch) thin Chinese egg
    noodles, preferably fresh

1 In a food processor fitted with a metal blade or in blender, combine sauce ingredients until smooth. Add enough water so that mixture will fall from a spoon in wide, silky ribbons. Adjust seasoning to taste. Transfer mixture to bowl and seal airtight. Set aside at room temperature. (This can be made several hours in advance or refrigerated overnight. Bring to room temperature before using.)
2 Bring 4½ ltrs (8 pts) unsalted water to a rolling boil in stock-pot or Dutch oven.
3 Toast sesame seeds in small, heavy skillet over medium heat, stirring until golden, about 3 minutes. Remove to plate to cool.

4 If using fresh noodles, fluff them to separate strands before adding to pot. Using wooden chopsticks or 2 long-handled wooden spoons, swish noodles gently back and forth several times to separate strands. Cook fresh noodles 1 to 2 minutes, until a single strand tastes cooked but still firm to a bite. Cook 4 to 8 minutes more if using dried noodles.
5 Drain immediately in colander and flush with cold running water until noodles are thoroughly chilled, tossing them gently to cool them quickly and evenly. Shake well to remove excess water.
6 Dry pot and return noodles to it.
7 Stir sauce. If it thickened when refrigerated, blend in a bit more water to achieve ribbony consistency. Do not thin sauce too much; it should cling to the noodles.
8 Pour half the sauce over the noodles and with your hands or wooden spoons toss gently to coat and separate each strand. Do not break the noodles (which to Chinese are emblematic of long life). Pour remaining sauce into small bowl and serve immediately.
9 Just before serving, toss noodles to redistribute sauce. Serve on individual plates or in shallow pasta bowls and sprinkle toasted sesame seeds on top.

Steamed Spicy Fish with Black Mushrooms
Temple Fried Rice
Cold-Tossed Watercress with Sesame Seeds

A long, oval platter makes the best setting for a whole steamed fish. Use a broad server, which both cuts and lifts, for slicing and serving the fish. Serve the watercress on individual plates, if you wish.

Ideal for a summer evening, this elegant meal of steamed fish, fried rice, and watercress salad depends (as do all the menus in this book) on fresh ingredients simply prepared. When you buy the fish, choose a whole one with bright red gills and glassy black eyes, as these are signs of freshness. Be sure to have the scales, fins, gills and guts – including the air bladder – removed, but ask the fishmonger to leave the head and tail intact. If you cannot find a small, whole fish, use a 1 Kg (2 lb) section of a larger fish and have it cut in half lengthwise, through the backbone, so that you can lay it in the steamer skin side up as if it were two fish. Score the skin side only.

Temple fried rice is a vegetarian dish, common to Buddhist temple kitchens. Since Buddhists are vegetarians who omit strongly flavoured foods from their diets, this dish omits the meat, onions, and scallions that are typical ingredients in fried rice. Its unusual savouriness comes from celery heart, carrots, pine nuts, and eggs.

The watercress salad, briefly cooked, is a northern dish. Buy the crispest watercress you can find: good produce markets keep it standing in cold water or on shaved ice.

What to drink
Although Chinese food usually calls for a slightly sweet wine, a drier white would taste good here because of the savoury rice and egg dish. Try either an Alsation Sylvaner or a crisp Soave from Italy.

Start-to-Finish Steps
1 For fried rice recipe, follow rice recipe steps 1 and 2.
2 Bring to a boil 1 cup water. Follow fish recipe step 1.
3 Follow fish recipe steps 2 and 3, and fried rice recipe steps 1 and 2.
4 Follow watercress recipe steps 2 and 3.
5 Follow watercress recipe step 4 and fried rice recipe step 3.
6 Follow watercress recipe steps 5 through 7.
7 Follow fish recipe steps 4 through 8.
8 Follow watercress recipe step 8.
9 Follow fish recipe steps 9 through 11.
10 Complete rice recipe step 3.
11 Follow fish recipe step 12. While fish is steaming, beat eggs for fried rice recipe and follow step 4. Remove cover on cooked rice, step 4.
12 Follow fried rice recipe steps 5 through 8 and watercress recipe step 9.
13 Complete fried rice recipe steps 9 and 10, and fish recipe step 10. Serve at once.

Steamed Spicy Fish with Black Mushrooms and Ham

6 to 8 Chinese dried black mushrooms
1.5 Kg (3 lb) fresh whole fish (pompano, sea bass, porgy, flounder, or wall-eye), cleaned and gutted, with head and tail left on
30 g (1 oz) Smithfield ham or prosciutto, cut into paper-thin slices
2 teaspoons coarse salt
2 tablespoons Chinese rice wine or dry sherry
2 tablespoons light soy sauce
2 teaspoons sesame oil
$^1/_4$ teaspoon sugar
2 teaspoons garlic, finely minced (about 2 cloves)
$1^1/_2$ teaspoons finely minced fresh ginger
$^1/_2$ teaspoon dried red pepper flakes
3 tablespoons thinly sliced scallion

1 Cover mushrooms with boiling water and allow to soak 20 to 30 minutes.
2 Trim fat from ham or prosciutto. Mince fat and reserve about 1 scant tablespoon. Cut ham into pieces about $2^1/_2$ cm (1 inch) square.
3 Rinse fish clean with water, inside and out. Shake to remove excess water, then pat fish dry inside and out with paper towels.
4 Holding cleaver or knife at a 45-degree angle, score fish at $2^1/_2$ cm (1 inch) intervals from neck to tail on both sides. Follow natural curve of collar and extend each cut from dorsal to ventral sides of fish (that is, from top to belly), cutting down nearly to the bone.

5 Sprinkle salt evenly over outside and inside of fish. Gently rub salt in score marks.
6 Put fish on heatproof oval platter about $2^1/_2$ cm (1 inch) smaller than fish steamer or large sauté pan. (If using bamboo steamer.)
7 In small bowl, stir to combine wine, soy sauce, sesame oil, and sugar. Add garlic and ginger, and stir to blend. Pour mixture over fish.

8 In another bowl, combine reserved minced fat, red pepper flakes, and scallion rings. Sprinkle over fish.

9 Drain mushrooms and, using scissors, snip off stems and cut caps in half. Rinse caps under cold running water to dislodge any sand.

10 Neatly arrange ham and mushrooms along cuts in fish. Seal platter with plastic wrap.

11 Bring hot water to a gushing boil in covered steamer or large sauté pan. The water should not touch platter on which fish will steam.

12 Remove plastic wrap and put platter with fish on steaming rack or trivet. Wait until steam surges around fish, then reduce heat to medium-high and cover pan. Steam fish 10 to 15 minutes, depending on thickness of fish, or until flesh at base of score marks is white and firm. Do not overcook, as the fish will continue to cook from its own heat when it is removed from burner.

13 If fish was cooked in steamer, bring steamer directly to the table on a tray. Otherwise, lift out serving plate and place on serving trivet at the table.

Temple Fried Rice

2 medium-size carrots, peeled and trimmed
1 celery heart, plus several trimmed inner stalks
60 g (2 oz) pine nuts
4^1/$_2$ to 5 tablespoons corn or peanut oil
3 large eggs, beaten
2 teaspoons Chinese rice wine or dry sherry
625 g (1^1/$_4$ lb) cooked rice, at room temperature
1 teaspoon coarse salt or 2 tablespoons light soy sauce

1 Cut carrots lengthwise in half. Lay halves flat and cut lengthwise in half again. Firmly grasp the pieces together and cut crosswise into small, fan-shaped pieces, about 2^1/$_2$ mm (^{1}/$_8$ inch) thick. Put in small bowl.

2 Cut celery heart, leaves and all, into thin slices. Cut celery stalks lengthwise into fourths. Firmly grasp the pieces together in tight bunch and cut them crosswise into thin arcs. Measure out about 60 g (2 oz) and reserve in small bowl.

3 Toast pine nuts in small heavy skillet until fragrant and lightly golden, about 2 to 3 minutes on medium to medium-high heat. Shake pan so nuts do not brown. Pour nuts into saucer and set aside.

4 Heat a wok or skillet over high heat until hot enough to evaporate a bead of water on contact. Add 2^1/$_2$ tablespoons oil and swirl to coat pan. Reduce heat to medium-high and add beaten eggs to pan. They should puff and bubble immediately. Pause 2 to 3 seconds until a film of cooked egg sets on bottom, then tip pan toward you and with wooden spoon push cooked egg away. Pause about 2 seconds for a new film to set on bottom, then push it to far side of pan. Continue cooking until there is no more flowing egg. Turn out soft mass onto flat plate and dice into small bites or slivers. The egg should be moist, yellow, and loosely set. It will cook to doneness when combined with rice.

5 Heat wok or heavy skillet over medium-high heat until hot enough to evaporate a bead of water on contact. Add 2 tablespoons oil, swirling to coat bottom. When oil is hot, add carrots and stir-fry briskly, about 15 seconds, in order to glaze pieces with oil and heat them through.

6 Add celery and toss briskly about 10 seconds. Scatter wine (or sherry) into pan and toss quickly just to mix.

7 Immediately add rice and toss briskly to combine. Lower heat if rice begins to scorch and drizzle in a bit more oil from the side if rice is sticking badly (it does tend to stick a little bit). Continue tossing until rice is heated through.

8 Sprinkle salt or soy sauce over rice and toss briskly to blend. Then taste, adding more seasoning if needed.

9 Return eggs to pan and toss gently 10 seconds just to combine and heat through.

10 Put rice in serving bowl and scatter in pine nuts. Toss gently to combine.

Cold-Tossed Watercress with Sesame Seeds

4 bunches fresh watercress (about 750 g (1¹/₂ lb))
2 teaspoons raw or black sesame seeds
4 teaspoons sugar
5 teaspoons sesame oil
2 teaspoons light soy sauce
2 teaspoons unseasoned Oriental rice vinegar

1   Bring 4¹/₂ ltrs (8 pts) unsalted water to a boil in a large stockpot or Dutch oven
2   Cut watercress above band that joins each band and discard stems. Discard any wilted or discoloured pieces from leafy tops.
3   Fill large mixing bowl with cold water and add watercress. Pump up and down with your hand to dislodge any dirt. Drain in colander, then shake off excess water. Dry bowl.
4   If using raw sesame seeds, toast them in a small heavy skillet over medium heat, stirring until golden, about 3 minutes. Put seeds aside to saucer to cool. Black seeds do not require toasting.
5   Add watercress to the boiling water, pushing leaves beneath surface with spatula. Blanch 20 seconds, then drain immediately in colander and flush with cold running water until chilled.
6   Using your hands, press down gently but firmly to remove excess water, then sandwhich watercress between two triple thicknesses of paper towels and pat dry.
7   Transfer watercress to the large mixing bowl. Fluff mass with your fingers and gently separate leaves.
8   Whisk sugar, sesame oil, soy sauce, and rice vinegar in small bowl, stirring briskly to thicken mixture. Taste and adjust with a bit more sugar, if desired. Pour sauce over watercress and with your fingers toss well to coat leaves. Cover with plastic wrap and chill.
9   Just before serving, toss watercress to redistribute seasonings. Mound on plate or in shallow bowl of contrasting colour, then sprinkle sesame seeds on top.

Added touch

For a fruit compote that will satisfyingly end this meal, peel and section one large grapefruit and four medium oranges, reserving their juice. Arrange the fruit in 4 serving dishes and drizzle the juice over them. Serve plain, or top with blueberries or whole strawberries, if in season. Sliced fresh kiwi fruit is also good, and you might combine it with lemon, lime, or tangerine sherbet.

Audrey and Calvin Lee

Menu 1
(*left*)
Seafood Treasure Noodles
Shantung Chicken with Hot Hoison
Sauce

Chinese cooks frequently combine the full range of Chinese regional cooking techniques – braising, poaching, steaming, deep frying, and stir-frying – when preparing an entire meal, and often they use two or three techniques within a single recipe. Such diversity has long appealed to Calvin and Audrey Lee.

Mr. Lee's heritage and training – in a family-owned restaurant – are Cantonese, but he has enjoyed experimenting with all of China's regional dishes. Mrs. Lee emphasizes the importance of visual impact and urges you to take time to arrange the food carefully on the serving platter with such garnishes as toasted sesame seeds or chipped scallions. Together the Lees believe in the merits of each region's style of cooking, so they have borrowed from all to develop their own particular approach.

Each of their menus is suitable for serving either family or guests because they are all exceptionally attractive yet simple to prepare. In the Cantonese-style Menu 1, a medley of seafood rest on cooked noodles – a Chinese favourite often served as part of the main meal or between meals as a substantial snack. In Menu 2, the ingredients suggest the name of the dish, *lions head:* meatballs representing the lion's head , the vegetable its mane. The duck in Menu 3 cooks in a savoury sauce and arrives at the table with a pungent asparagus salad and delicate corn soup.

A noodle dish of stir-fried scallops, shrimp, and squid, if you wish, pairs beautifully with the richly coloured chicken in hot hoisin sauce. Pass a bowl of sliced scallions so that guests can add them as a garnish to the seafood.

Seafood Treasure Noodles
Shantung Chicken with Hot Hoisin Sauce

The focal point of this substantial meal is the stir-fried seafood on a bed of noodles, a dish that is a year-round Chinese favourite. Beacause of their length, noodles are symbols of longevity to the Chinese, who have invented endless variations on the noodle theme. Oriental noodles are made with eggs and wheat or rice flours, and come in a variety of shapes. Whether you buy fresh or dried Oriental noodles for this recipe, you must boil them first and then let them drain before stir-frying them. For this recipe, you form the cooked noodles into four pancakes, then fry them on each side until they are crispy brown. You may use spaghetti or vermicelli instead.

A medley of fresh seafood – shrimp, scallops, and, if you wish, squid – are sweet and flavourful topping for the noodles. You stir fry the seafood with broccoli, snow peas, water chestnuts, and straw mushrooms, then blend them with oyster sauce, which unifies the seafood flavours.

The sweet yet spicy chicken with *hoisin* sauce is an accent dish, a counterpoint to the sweet seafood. The *hoisin* sauce is sweet, and the dried red pepper flakes spicy hot.

What to drink

The cooks suggest a dry white wine with a medium body to accompany this menu – either a French Graves or a dry California Sauvignon blanc, for example.

Start-to-Finish Steps

1. Bring 3³/₄ ltrs (6 pts) water to a boil for noodles recipe step 1.
2. Follow Shantung chicken recipe steps 1 and 2.
3. Follow noodle recipe steps 2 through 8.
4. Preheat oven to 200°C (400°F or Mark 6) and follow Shantung chicken recipe steps 3 through 7.
5. Wipe out pan. Follow noodles recipe steps 9 through 15. Remove chicken from oven and serve.

Seafood Treasure Noodles

250 g (8 oz) thin Chinese egg noodles or vermicelli
1 bunch broccoli (about 750 g (1¹/₂ lb))
125 g (4 oz) fresh snow peas
500 g (1 lb) canned straw mushrooms
250 g (8 oz) canned water chestnuts, drained
4 scallions
250 g (8 oz) medium shrimp (about 8 to 10)
250 g (8 oz) bay or sea scallops
1 small squid, cleaned (optional)
6 tablespoons peanut oil
salt
2 slices fresh ginger, 2 cm (³/₄ inch) square
2 teaspoons dry sherry
2 tablespoons water
3 tablespoons oyster sauce
2 teaspoons Oriental sesame oil

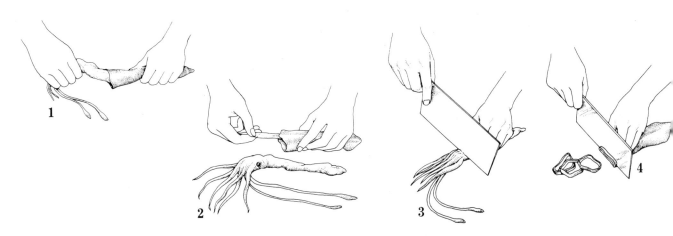

1   Bring stockpot or kettle of water to a boil over high heat.

2   Add noodles and cook 5 minutes, or until noodles are firm to the bite. Drain in colander and rinse under cold running water. Pat dry. Divide into 4 mounds.

3   Cut broccoli into florets 5 cm (2 inches) long. Peel stems so they are about 5 mm ($^1/_4$ inch) thick.

4   String snow peas and set aside in bowl. Drain straw mushrooms and add to the snow peas. Slice each water chestnuts into $2^1/_2$ mm ($^1/_8$ inch) ovals and add to the vegetables.

5   Slice scallions, including the green, into 5 mm ($^1/_4$ inch) lengths and put aside separately for garnish.

6   Peel shrimp. Using small sharp knife, slice halfway through back of each shrimp and remove black vein. Shrimp will curl prettily when cooked.

7   Rinse scallops. If using sea scallops, quarter each one. If using bay scallops, leave them whole.

8   If using squid, first hold head with one hand and body with the other, and firmly pull head from body sac. Next, take hold of quill-like piece located at top of body sac and remove it by pulling. Make sure you get rid of all of it, as it may break into smaller pieces. Peel away the black-flecked skin and rinse squid. Cut away tentacles and leave whole. Slice body into very thin rings.

9   Heat wok or large, heavy skillet over high heat. Add 2 tablespoons peanut oil and $^1/_4$ teaspoon salt, and stir to coat pan. when oil is quite hot, add the 4 mounds of noodles. Press down firmly on each mound with back of metal spatula to form 4 pancakes about 1 cm ($^1/_2$ inch) thick.

10 Pan fry the noodle pancakes 2 minutes, or until light brown and crusty. Turn pancakes and brown other side 2 minutes. Remove to serving platter lined with paper towels to drain; keep warm.

11 Wipe out pan with paper towels. Add 2 tablespoons peanut oil to pan and heat until almost smoking. Add $^1/_4$ teaspoon salt and ginger. Stir to distribute oil. Add shrimp and squid. Stir 1 minute. Add half the sherry and stir briefly just until shrimp turn pink. Repeat process for scallops and cook until opaque. Remove scallops to bowl and discard ginger.

12 Wipe out pan with paper towels and reheat over high heat. Add 2 tablespoons peanut oil and $^1/_4$ teaspoon salt. When oil is almost smoking, add broccoli and stir 1 minute. Add snow peas, straw mushrooms, and water chestnuts, and cook, stirring, 1 minute. Add water, cover pan, and cook 2 minutes.

13 Uncover and return seafood to pan. Stir to mix with the vegetables. Add oyster sauce and stir to blend.

14 Remove pan from heat and stir in sesame oil.

15 Place equal portions of seafood mixture on each noodle pancake and serve immediately with garnish of chopped scallions on the side.

Shantung Chicken with Hot Hoisin Sauce

500 g (1 lb) skinless, boneless chicken breasts (about 2 whole breasts)
2 tablespoons *hoisin* sauce
2 teaspoons dry sherry
1 tablespoon dark soy sauce
4 scallions
2 tablespoons peanut oil
$^1/_2$ teaspoon dried red pepper flakes
60 ml (2 fl oz) Chinese Chicken Stock

1   Cut chicken into 1 cm ($^1/_2$ inch) squares.

2   Combine hoisin sauce, sherry, and soy sauce in mixing bowl. Add chicken and coat well with sauce. Let chicken marinate until ready to cook.

3   Slice scallions into 1 cm ($^1/_2$ inch) lengths. Set aside for garnish.

4   Heat wok or skillet over high heat. Add oil and red pepper flakes, and stir briefly to distribute oil in pan. When oil is almost smoking, carefully add chicken and marinade. Stir-fry vigorously 1 minute.

5   Carefully add chicken stock and stir quickly to blend. Cover and cook 2 minutes.

6   Uncover and cook a few minutes more to reduce sauce slightly, stirring constantly.

7   Remove to serving dish and garnish with the scallions. Keep warm in preheated slow oven.

Menu 2

Lion's Head
Stir-Fried Cauliflower and Sweet Peppers
Rice

Heavy white pottery bowls make perfect serving pieces for this attractive but simple dinner. The braised meatballs mimic lions' heads, and the cooked spinach leaves are the manes. Cauliflower and red pepper add a color contrast.

The lion's head recipe exemplifies the Chinese delight in symbolism and the use of whimsical names. The original recipe calls for huge meatballs, but here the Lees have made them smaller in the interest of cooking speed and have substituted spinach for the more traditional Chinese cabbage.

Stir-fried cauliflower and slices of red pepper are lightly seasoned with fresh ginger, soy sauce , and sesame oil.

The Lees include their special method of treating rice. Washing and rinsing rice until the water runs clear ia a ritual in Chinese kitchens, and is thought to tenderise rice and improve taste.

What to drink

The cooks recommend an imported beer for this meal, and they prefer the dark and malty variety to light lagers. Several Mexican beers, some dark German beers, and some of the darker English ales would be ideal.

Start-to-Finish Steps

1 Follow rice recipe steps 1 and 2.
2 Follow lion's head recipe steps 1 and 2.
3 Follow rice recipe step 3 and lion's head recipe steps 3 through 7.
4 Preheat oven to 200°C (400°F or Mark 6). Follow stir-fried cauliflower recipe steps 1 and 2.
5 Complete lion's head recipe, steps 8 through 10.
6 Follow rice recipe step 4 and cauliflower recipe steps 3 through 6. Remove lion's head dish from oven and serve.

Lion's Head

750 g (1¹/₂ lb) fresh spinach
12 water chestnuts
3¹/₂ cm (1¹/₂ inch) knob fresh ginger
4 scallions, trimmed
500 g (1 lb) ground pork
1 egg
¹/₂ teaspoon sesame oil
2 teaspoons dry sherry
3 tablespoons dark soy sauce

1 tablespoon plus 2 teaspoons cornstarch
125 ml (4 fl oz) peanut oil
125 ml (4 fl oz) Chinese Chicken Stock or canned broth
$^1/_2$ teaspoon sugar

1 Wash spinach and trim off tough stems. Drain leaves well in colander. Pat dry with paper towels.
2 Using food processor fitted with steel blade or using a knife, mince water chestnuts. Peel and mince fresh ginger to measure about 2 tablespoons. Remove root ends and slice scallions into thin rounds. Combine water chestnuts, scallions, ginger, and ground meat in large bowl.
3 Beat egg in small bowl and add it to pork mixture along with sesame oil, sherry, and 1 tablespoon dark soy sauce. Sprinkle with 1 tablespoon cornstarch.
4 Blend mixture well and form into 16 meatballs about $3^1/_2$ cm ($1^1/_2$ inch) in diameter.
5 Heat peanut oil in Dutch oven or flameproof casserole until it is almost smoking. Add meatballs and brown thoroughly, about 6 to 8 minutes.
6 Meanwhile, combine chicken stock or broth, remaining dark soy sauce, and sugar in small cup.
7 When meatballs have browned, remove them with slotted spoon to platter and pour off oil. Add chicken stock mixture to Dutch oven or casserole and bring to a boil. Return meatballs to pot. Cover and regulate heat so that liquid bibbles steadily.
8 After meatballs have cooked 10 to 15 minutes, uncover and place spinach on top of meatballs. Replace lid firmly. Raise heat and steam 3 to 5 minutes, or until done.
9 Remove spinach with slotted spoon and arrange on shallow serving dish. Arrange meatballs on top of spinach.
10 Bring leftover cooking liquid to a boil. Combine remaining cornstarch with 1 tablespoon water and add to sauce in pan. Stir vigorously until thickened. Pour sauce over meatballs and spinach. Keep warm until ready to serve.

Stir-Fried Cauliflower and Sweet Peppers

1 small head cauliflower (about 500 g (1 lb))
1 large red pepper
1 cm ($^3/_4$ inch) square slices fresh ginger
60 ml (2 fl oz) Chinese Chicken Stock
$^1/_2$ teaspoon light soy sauce
2 tablespoons peanut oil
$^1/_2$ teaspoon salt
$^1/_2$ teaspoon sesame oil

1 Cut cauliflower into florets approximately $3^1/_2$ cm ($1^1/_2$ inch) across. Discard green leaves. Core and remove seeds from pepper; slice lengthwise into 1 cm ($^1/_2$ inch) strips. Slice fresh ginger.
2 In measuring cup, combine chicken stock and light soy sauce.
3 Heat oil in wok or large heavy skillet until very hot. Maintain high heat throughout cooking process. Add salt and ginger. Stir 10 seconds.
4 Add cauliflower and pepper. Stir 1 minute.
5 Add chicken stock mixture and stir to coat vegetables. Cover pan and cook 2 to 5 minutes.
6 Remove pan from heat and stir in sesame oil. Serve immediately.

Rice

300 g (10 oz) long-grain rice
625 ml ($1^1/_4$ pts) water

1 Wash rice by rubbing it between your hands in several changes of water to remove any excess starch.
2 Combine rice and water in $1^1/_2$ ltr (3 pt) saucepan. Bring to a boil over high heat. Continue to boil rice, uncovered, about 5 minutes, until virtually all visible water has evaporated, leaving bubbles and air holes on surface of rice.
3 Cover pan and simmer over very low heat 18 or 20 minutes.
4 Uncover and stir well to fluff rice before serving.

<table>
<tr><td>

Menu

___

3

</td><td>

Corn Soup
Red-Cooked Duck
Asparagus Salad/Rice

</td></tr>
</table>

One of the hallmarks of Shanghai or Eastern-style cooking is the red-cooking method – a method involving the use of dark brown soy sauce in a liquid to braise, or slow-cook, a meat until it is tender. The soy sauce is what gives the meat its reddish colour. This technique

Corn soup, red-cooked duck, steamed rice, and an asparagus salad served on traditional Chinese dinnerware look at home in a dramatic table setting.

adapts equally well to meat , poultry, and seafood, whether cooked whole or chopped into smaller portions. And the cooking broth, which you can strain and refrigerate for re-use, improves with age.

Normally this method requires several hours of cooking time, but the quartered duck in this recipe cooks through quickly. The market for duck has grown rapidly in the last few years, and fresh ducks – as well as frozen – are increasingly available from meat markets

and some supermarkets. To get a fresh duck, you may need to notify your butcher a couple of days in advance. If you buy a frozen duck, check the expiration date on the package.

The Lees call for a heavy cleaver for cutting off the wing tips and quartering the duck. A chef's knife will also do the work, or you can ask the butcher to quarter the duck when you buy it. At this meal you probably should give your guests the option of using a knife and fork instead of chopsticks, since picking meat off the bones with a pair of chopsticks requires a certain dexterity. However, this braised duck is so tender that the meat comes off the bone with little difficulty.

You can make the asparagus salad ahead and serve it either at room temperature or slightly chilled. The dressing, a Chinese version of a French Vinaigrette, is particularly good with the rich-tasting duck. Always use fresh asparagus. If the season is past , however, you may substitue green beans. Cook them exactly as you would the asparagus and use the same dressing.

The creamy corn soup takes only minutes to prepare; flavoured with chicken and ham, it is particularly delicious with chicken or duck.

What to drink
With this menu, try either a light red wine, such as a Beaujolais or a young Chianti, or a fuller-boddied wine, such as a California or Alsation gewürztraminer. The cooks do not recommend beer, but Calvin Lee's personal choice, rather than wine, is a single dry martini, served very cold.

Start-to-Finish Steps

1 Cut scallions into 2.5 cm (1 inch) thick lengths and follow red-cooked duck recipe steps 1 through 4.

2 While duck is cooking, follow rice recipe steps 1 and 2.

3 Follow corn soup recipe steps 1 through 3.

4 Follow duck recipe step 5 and rice recipe step 3.

5 Follow soup recipe step 4 and asparagus recipe steps 1 through 5.

6 Follow soup recipe steps 5 and 6 and red-cooked duck recipe steps 6 and 7.

7 Complete asparagus recipe, steps 6 and 7, rice recipe step 4, and serve.

Corn Soup

300 g (10 oz) package frozen corn
250 ml (8 fl oz) milk
2 Kg (4 lb) skinless, boneless chicken breast
1 ltr (1³/₄ pts) plus 3 tablespoons water
250 ml (8 fl oz) Chinese Chicken Stock
2 teaspoons salt
2 teaspoons sugar
8-inch slice Smithfield or Westphalian ham
1 teaspoon cornstarch
1 egg white

1 In medium-size saucepan of boiling water to cover, cook package of corn 5 minutes. Remove from heat and drain pan. Open package, return contents to pan, and simmer with 250 ml (8 fl oz) milk until tender.

2 In food processor fitted with steel blade, puree chicken. Or mince chicken, first using sharp edge and then using blunt edge of knife. Combine with 1 ltr (1³/₄ pts) water in small bowl. Set aside.

3 Combine chicken stock, salt, and sugar with the corn in saucepan and bring to a boil over medium heat, stirring occasionally.

4 Mince ham and add to soup along with minced chicken mixture. Simmer, stirring , 2 minutes.

5 Mix cornstarch with 3 tablespoons water in measuring cup. Slowly add cornstarch mixture to soup. Cook, stirring, to thicken slightly. Remove from heat.

6 Beat egg white in medium-size bowl with fork or whisk until light and foamy. Stirring constantly, drizzle egg white into hot soup to form long, thin threads. Keep warm until ready to serve, but do not allow to boil.

Red-Cooked Duck

250 ml (8 fl oz) dark soy sauce
250 ml (8 fl oz) light soy sauce
250 ml (8 fl oz) water
1 Kg (2 lb) sugar
2 star anise (16 sections)
2 Kg (4 lb) duckling
4 scallions, cut into thirds

1 In a wok or 6 ltr (10 pint) Dutch oven, combine all ingredients except duck and scallions, and bring to a boil.

2 Remove any excess fat from cavity of duck. Trim off neck skin. Chop off wing tips and save the neck and gizzards for future use. With heavy cleaver, quarter duck: Place duck breast side up and cut through keel bone. Push back breast halves and cut back bone in two. Next, place each body piece skin side up on cutting surface and, feeling for end of rib cage, cut each piece in half. Turn quarters skin side down and, with sharp knife or cleaver, trim skin and any visible fat from edges of each piece. Turn pieces

over and prick lightly with prongs of sharp fork to help duck release its fat during cooking.

3 Place duck quarters skin side down in pot. Spoon sauce over duck, add scallions, and cover. Regulate heat so that sauce bubbles steadily at a slow boil or high simmer.

4 Cook duck 20 minutes. Turn pieces over and cook another 20 to 25 minutes.

5 When duck is done (flesh should feel slightly resilient to the touch), remove it to a chopping block and let it rest at least 5 minutes.

6 Ladle approximately 250 ml (8 fl oz) of the cooking liquid into fat separator or medium-size bowl. Let fat rise to top and discard. The degreased sauce may be put in small bowl and used as dipping sauce for duck at the table. Or, some of the sauce may be drizzled over duck before serving.

7 Remove wings and legs from duck with heavy cleaver. Chop legs crosswise at 5 cm (2 inch) intervals. Do same with breast pieces. Serve garnished with scallions.

Asparagus Salad

24 asparagus spears, about 5 cm (2 inches) in diameter
1 tablespoon dark soy sauce
2 teaspoons Oriental sesame oil
1 teaspoon Chinese rice wine vinegar
1 teaspoon Sugar
1 teaspoon raw sesame seeds

1 Bring 1¼ ltrs (2 pts) water to a boil in a covered stockpot or kettle.

2 Wash asparagus and snap off any white woody ends. Slice stalks diagonally at 5 cm (2 inch) intervals.

3 When water comes to a rolling boil, uncover pot and add asparagus. Cook 1 minute, or until just barely cooked and still crisp. Do not overcook.

4 Drain asparagus in colander under very cold running water to stop cooking as quickly as possible. Toss with 2 large wooden spoons to hasten cooling.

5 When cool, blot off any excess moisture and place in serving dish.

6 Whisk together soy sauce, sesame oil, vinegar, and sugar in small bowl until sugar is dissolved. Pour over asparagus.

7 Toast sesame seeds in small ungreased skillet over moderately high heat. Shake pan until they are

Rice

300 g (10 oz) long-grain rice
625 ml (1¼ pts) water

1 Wash rice by rubbing it between your hands in several changes of water to remove any excess starch.

2 Combine rice and water in 1½ ltr (3 pt) saucepan. Bring to a boil over high heat. Continue to boil rice, uncovered, about 5 minutes, until virtually all visible water has evaporated, leaving bubbles and air holes on surface of rice.

3 Cover pan and simmer over very low heat 18 or 20 minutes.

4 Uncover and stir well to fluff rice before serving.

Nina Simonds

Menu 1
(left)
Drunken Mushrooms
Baked Fish Packages with Ham and
Mushrooms
Stir-Fried Lettuce
Rice

The land of rice and fish' is the local name for the fertile region along China's Eastern seacoast, which includes the provinces of Chekiang, Kiangsu, Fukien, and the cosmopolitian city of Shanghai. Seafood, fresh vegetables, meat, poultry, rice, and wheat products, liberally seasoned with soy sauce and red wine, characterize this style of cooking. Typical of the East, too, is the well-known 'red-cooking' method, which involves simmering meats or poultry in a soy-based broth for a rich, flavourful stew.

Nina Simonds, cookbook auther and teacher, is a particular admirer of the Shanghai style. She learned its secret not on the mainland but on the island of Taiwan, where she apprenticed to a chef for three and a half years. Like most good cooks, however, she likes and uses Cantonese recipes, too, as well as the hot spices of the West.

Menu 1, parchment-wrapped fish and mushrooms cooked in wine, is a delicately flavoured Eastern-style meal. Menu 2 is a contrast: spicy spareribs, a noodle salad, and stir-fried cucumbers, all from Szechwan and Hunan. Menu 3 pairs marinated chicken shreds wrapped in lettuce leaves with another southern dish – barbacued chicken livers and water chestnuts.

When you serve the fish wrapped in paper, bring each package to the table unopened. When guests unwrap their portions, they will appreciate the burst of fragrant aroma. Serve the whole mushrooms on a nest of quickly stir-fried lettuce.

Menu 1

Drunken Mushrooms
Baked Fish Packages with Ham and Mushroom
Stir-Fried Lettuce/Rice

This Eastern-style meal offers an adaptation of a Chinese favourite – food cooked in paper wrapping. Meats or fish folded in parchment or rice paper cook quickly while basting in their own juices. To finish preparing the fish and its accompaniments in this recipe, wrap all in a small square of kitchen parchment, which you can buy in hardware stores or, occasionally, in supermarkets. You may also use clean brown wrapping paper lightly oiled or aluminium foil.

To serve, loosen the paper or foil but do not remove it. You and your guests can pick out each bite with a fork or chopsticks. To cut the time you spend in the kitchen after your guests arrive, wrap the packets several hours in advance of dinner time and refrigerate them. Be sure to bring them to room temperature before baking.

In this particular recipe, the cured ham slivers add zest to the bland fish. In China, Chinese *jinhua* ham, which has a deep scarlet colour and a pungent smoky taste, is traditionally used. However, Smithfield ham or prosciutto is more easily available here and is very good in this recipe. Black mushrooms have a woodlike flavour that blends well with rice wine, ginger, and scallions. Rice wine is a staple on Chinese shelves, and cooks use it in many sauces for a last-minute dash of flavour. Nina Simonds prefers using Scotch as a substitute for rice wine instead of the more familiar dry sherry.

As the name implies, 'drunken' dishes always feature a generous amount of wine with seafood, chicken, or other meats or, in this menu, mushrooms. Here the button mushrooms steep in the wine-enriched chicken stock and absorb the flavours of the garlic, scallions, and ginger. Because the flavour of the wine is so prominent in this recipe, use a good-quality rice wine such as *shaosing*. Otherwise, substitute a half portion of Scotch.

Both recipes call for fresh ginger, an indispensable ingredient in all Chinese cooking. Ground or candied ginger is no substitute for fresh, but fortunately fresh ginger is available in most well-stocked supermarkets and at green grocers. As the pantry section directs, always select a firm, pale brown root. If the ginger you buy is wrinkled or soft, it will not have its sharp clean taste, and you will need to use more ginger in your recipe. If your ginger is properly fresh, you do not need to peel it for mincing or chopping. For short-term storage, keep it in a cool, dry place. Otherwise

wrap it tightly in foil or a plastic bag and refrigerate it. You may also peel it and put it in an airtight glass jar with enough rice wine or sherry to cover it.

What to drink
The delicate flavours of these dishes call for a good German Riesling, such as a Bernkasteler or Piesporter.

Start-toFinish Steps
1 Follow rice recipe steps 1 and 2.
2 Follow baked fish recipe steps 1 and 2.
3 Follow stir-fried lettuce recipe steps 1 and 2, and drunken mushrooms steps 1 and 2.
4 Follow baked fish recipe steps 3 through 8.
5 Follow drunken mushrooms recipe step 3.
6 Wipe out pan and follow stir-fried lettuce recipe step 3.
7 Follow drunken mushrooms recipe step 4 and rice recipe step 3.
8 Complete stir-fried lettuce recipe step 4, baked fish recipe step 9, rice recipe step 4, and drunken mushrooms recipe step 5. Serve.

Drunken Mushrooms

4 cloves garlic
4 scallions
6 slices fresh ginger, 1 cm (3/4 inch) square
1 cup good quality Chinese rice wine or 1/2 cup Scotch
350 ml (12 fl oz) Chinese Chicken Stock, or 500 ml (1 pt) if using Scotch
1 teaspoon salt
500 g (1 lb) fresh mushrooms
Juice of 1/2 lemon

1 Using flat side of cleaver or chef's knife, lightly crush garlic cloves, scallions, and fresh ginger.
2 Place all ingredients except mushrooms and lemon juice in heavy saucepan and bring to a boil. Boil mixture vigorously about 5 minutes.
3 Lightly rinse mushrooms and drain thoroughly. Trim stem ends and cut large caps in half. Toss in medium-size bowl with lemon juice.

4   Add mushrooms to stock and cook about 2 minutes. Turn off heat and let sit until ready to serve. Can be served warm or at room temperature.

5   To serve at table, spoon mushrooms into centre of the beds of stir-fried lettuce. Sprinkle some of the broth on top.

Baked Fish Packages with Ham and Mushrooms

4 Chinese dried black mushrooms
4 fillets of sole or flounder (about 250 g (8 oz) each)

The marinade:
2 slices fresh ginger, 1 cm (³/₄ inch) crushed with flat side of cleaver
1 teaspoon salt
1 tablespoon Chinese rice wine or Scotch
The sauce:
1 tablespoon thin soy sauce
2 tablespoons Chinese rice wine or Scotch
1 teaspoon sugar
¹/₂ teaspoon salt
1 teaspoon sesame oil
1¹/₂ teaspoons cornstarch
60 ml (2 fl oz) Chinese Chicken Stock
1 tablespoon peanut, safflower, or corn oil
1 tablespoon minced scallions
2 teaspoons minced fresh ginger
2 paper-thin slices Smithfield ham or prosciutto (about 30–45 g (1–1¹/₂ oz), cut in half crosswise to make 4 pieces

1   In small bowl, cover mushrooms with boiling water and allow to soften 20 minutes.

2   Lightly rinse fillets and pat dry. Place on oval platter and cover with marinade ingredients until ready to cook.

3   Preheat oven to 230°C (450°F or Mark 8).

4   Combine sauce ingredients in bowl.

5   Remove mushrooms from water and squeeze out excess moisture. Remove and discard stems. Cut caps into matchstick-size shreds or into long strips.

6   Heat wok or heavy skillet, add cooking oil, and heat until very hot. Add minced scallions and ginger, and stir-fry about 10 seconds over high heat until fragrant. Add sauce and cook, stirring constantly, until thickened. Pour sauce back into bowl.

7   Lightly grease the squares of paper and fold in half diagonally. Open up and place 1 fish fillet on each square along the fold. Tuck ends of fillets under so that they are not too close to edge of paper.

Arrange 1 piece of ham in centre of each fillet. Sprinkle some of shredded mushroom on top and spoon one quarter of the sauce over all. Fold over each square to enclose the fillet and fold in edges of paper, pinching and tucking to make pleats. Repeat for remaining 3 packages.

8   Arrange packages, pleated edges up, on baking sheet. Bake packages 6 to 10 minutes, depending on thickness of fillets, or until fish flakes when prodded with a fork. (packages will be puffed up.)

9   Place 1 package on each plate and let each person cut open his package.

Stir-Fried Lettuce

2 large heads leaf lettuce
³/₄ teaspoon salt
1 tablespoon Chinese rice wine or Scotch
¹/₂ teaspoon sesame oil
1 tablespoon peanut, safflower, or corn oil

1   Lightly rinse lettuce in cold water and spin dry. Remove tough stems. Cut leaves into sections about 5 cm (2 inches) square.

2   Combine salt, wine, and sesame oil in bowl.

3   Heat wok or heavy skillet until very hot. Add cooking oil and heat until smoking. Add lettuce and sauce, and stir-fry, tossing constantly, over high heat 1 minute, or until lettuce is slightly wilted. Remove pan from heat.

4   Arrange equal portions of lettuce on one side of each dinner plate, making a slight depression in centre for the mushrooms.

Rice

300 g (10 oz) long-grain rice
625 ml (1¹/₄ pts) water

1   Wash rice by rubbing it between your hands in several changes of water to remove any excess starch.

2   Combine rice and water in 1¹/₂ ltr (3 pt) saucepan. Bring to a boil over high heat. Continue to boil rice, uncovered, about 5 minutes, until virtually all visible water has evaporated, leaving bubbles and air holes on surface of rice.

3   Cover pan and simmer over very low heat 18 or 20 minutes.

4   Uncover and stir well to fluff rice before serving.

<table>
<tr><td>Menu
2</td><td>**Spicy Braised Spareribs**
Tossed Noodle Salad
Stir-Fried Cucumbers with Peanut Sauce</td></tr>
</table>

To make the spicy spareribs in this menu, first deep fry them until they are golden brown and then braise, that is, slow-cook, them in a rich, spicy liquid. The braising liquid gradually reduces to a glaze, which coats and flavours the meat. Although the idea of braising meats is characteristic of Shanghai cooking – though not exclusive to the area – the spicing in this recipe (chili paste, scallions, and garlic) is Szechwan/Hunanese.

The Chinese do not eat Western-style salads with raw greens, but they do enjoy side dishes of cold dressed vegetables served alone or tossed with cooked noodles.

Stir-frying cucumbers may come as a new idea. To preserve the crispness and the decorative look, be sure to cook them very quickly over a high flame.

What to drink

This substantial menu needs a fuller-bodied, spicy wine like a Gewürztraminer. First choice here would be one from Alsace, but a California Gewürztraminer would also do.

Start-to-Finish Steps

In the morning: Lightly crush ginger, scallions, and garlic, and follow braised spareribs recipe step 1.
1   Follow braised spareribs recipe steps 2 through 5.
2   While spare ribs are cooking, prepare vegetables for noodle salad: rinse and drain sprouts, peel and shred carrots and courgettes, mince scallions.

Set out the spareribs and cucumbers on a dinner plate and, on a separate dish, carefully arrange the salad on a bed of noodles.

3   Follow noodle salad recipe steps 1 and 2.
4   Mince scallions and ginger for stir-fried cucumber recipe, then follow steps 1 and 2.
5   Follow noodle salad recipe steps 3 and 4.
6   Complete cucumber recipe step 4.
7   Wipe out pan. Follow noodle salad recipe step 5, braised spareribs recipe step 6, and serve.

Spicy Braised Spareribs

1.5 Kg (3 lb) counrty-style spareribs, cut into 6 cm (2$^1/_2$ inch) pieces
The Marinade:
1$^1/_2$ tablespoons thin soy sauce
1 tablespoon Chinese rice wine or Scotch
2 slices fresh ginger, lightly crushed
2 scallions, lightly crushed
2 cloves garlic, lightly crushed
The braising mixture:
60 ml (2 fl oz) Chinese rice wine or scotch
3 tablespoons thin soy sauce
3 tablespoons sugar
350 ml (12 fl oz) Chinese Chicken Stock
250 ml (8 fl oz) peanut, safflower, or corn oil
2 teaspoons chili paste
1 teaspoon sesame oil

1   Trim any excess fat from spareribs and place ribs in large bowl. Add marinade ingredients and turn ribs to coat with marinade. Cover bowl and refrigerate.
2   Combine braising mixture in small bowl.
3   Heat Dutch oven and add cooking oil. Heat oil to 200°C (400°F) on deep-fat thermometer and carefully place as many ribs in pan as will fit in one layer. Fry over high heat until golden brown on both sides, turning once. Remove with Chinese mesh spoon or long-handled slotted metal spoon and drain. Bring oil back to 200°C (400°F) and fry remaining ribs in same manner. Remove ribs. Carefully drain off hot oil.
4   Reheat pan and add chili paste. Stir fry several seconds over high heat. Add braising mixture and heat until boiling.
5   Add spareribs and return liquid to a boil. Reduce heat to medium and cook spareribs, partly covered, about 40 minutes, or until sauce is thick.
6   Add sesame oil and toss lightly before serving.

Tossed Noodle Salad

1 tablespoon peanut, safflower, or corn oil
250 g (8 oz) thin egg noodles
1$^1/_2$ tablespoons sesame oil
1 dried hot red pepper
250 g (8 oz) fresh mung bean sprouts , rinsed and drained

3 medium-size carrots, peeled and finely shredded 125 g (4 oz)
2 medium-size courgettes, finely shredded (125 g (4 oz))
2 tablespoons minced scallion
100 ml (3 fl oz) thin soy sauce
3 tablespoons Chinese rice wine
4 teaspoons sugar
2 tablespoons Chinese rice vinegar
1 tablespoon sesame oil
125 ml (4 fl oz) Chinese Chicken Stock or water

1   Bring 2$^1/_2$ ltrs (4 pts) water and cooking oil to a boil in stockpot. Add noodles and cook until just tender.
2   Drain in colander and rinse under cold water. Drain again, place in large deep bowl, and toss with sesame oil.
3   Wearing rubber gloves, carefully halve the hot pepper and remove seeds and membrane. Mince pepper and set aside.
4   Turn noodles out onto serving platter. Arrange bean sprouts, carrots, courgettes, and scallions in circles over the noodles.
5   Place pepper and remaining ingredients in wok or small saucepan and heat until boiling. Cook about 30 seconds to allow flavours to blend. Pour over noodles before serving.

Stir-Fried Cucumbers with Peanut Sauce

2 tablespoons smooth peanut butter
2 teaspoons thin soy sauce
2 teaspoons sugar
1$^1/_2$ tablespoons sesame oil
1$^1/_2$ teaspoons Chinese black vinegar
3 tablespoons Chinese Chicken Stock
2 large cucumbers, preferably seedless (1 Kg (2 lb))
2 tablespoons peanut, safflower, or corn oil
1 tablespoon minced scallions
2 teaspoons minced fresh ginger
1$^1/_2$ teaspoons chili paste
60 g (2 oz) roasted peanuts for garnish (optional)

1   Combine first 6 ingredients in small bowl.
2   Peel cucumbers and cut in half lengthwise. Scoop out seeds, if necessary, and cut each half lengthwise into quarters. Roll-cut quarters into 3$^1/_2$ cm (1$^1/_2$ inch) pieces.
3   Heat wok or skillet and add cooking oil. Heat until very hot. Add scallions and ginger, and stir-fry about 10 seconds, until fragrant. Add chili paste and stir-fry 5 seconds.
4   Add cucumbers and toss over high heat 1$^1/_2$ minutes. Add peanut sauce from step 1 and toss 15 seconds before serving. If desired, stir-fry peanuts 10 seconds and use as garnish.

Barbecued Chicken Livers
Shredded Chicken in Lettuce Packages
Rice

Shredded chicken and fried rice noodles nested in lettuce leaves are served with skewered chicken livers and vegetables.

The emphasis of Cantonese cooking is always on enhancing the flavour of the main ingredients, not overpowering it. Therefore, Cantonese chefs use chopped fresh ginger, minced garlic, and soy sauce – their basic flavouring agents – with care and restraint. The result is a much milder kind of cooking than the heartier, spicier Szechwan style. Cantonese cooking also tends to be less oily than any of the other regional styles.. This chicken liver recipe is a good example of southern Chinese cooking because the barbecue sauce is mild, and its ingredients complement the taste of the liver.

The second dish is marinated, shredded chicken strips deliciously combined with pine nuts, water chestnuts, and dried Chinese mushrooms and served over fried rice noodles nested in crisp lettuce leaves. Invite your guests to roll the leaves around the filling to make a Chinese-style sandwich.

The dried rice noodles, also known as maifun, that accompany the chicken add a delicious crunch to the 'sandwich.' The noodles expand when deep fried to become very light and crisp. Made from rice flour, they are popular in southern China, one of the nation's major rice-growing regions.

What to drink
A dry to slightly off-dry white wine will complement this meal. A California Sauvignon Blanc, a French Vouvray, or an Italian Pinot Grigio would all do nicely. More unusual but also very good would be a New York Seyval Blanc.

Start-to-Finish Steps
1 Follow shredded chicken recipe steps 1 through 3.
2 Follow chicken livers recipe steps 1 through 4.
3 Follow rice recipe (see page 9), steps 1 and 2.
4 Follow shredded chicken recipe steps 4 through 7.
5 Follow rice recipe step 3.
6 Follow shredded chicken recipe step 8.
7 Follow chicken livers recipe steps 5 through 7.
8 While chicken livers are grilling, complete shredded chicken recipe steps 9 through 11 and rice recipe step 4. Serve chicken livers, step 8, at once.

Barbecued Chicken Livers

12 canned water chestnuts, drained and halved
12 whole chicken livers (about 500 g (1 lb)), trimmed
    of fat
4 to 5 scallions, cut into 2½ cm (1 inch) lengths or
    longer
4 tablespoons *hoisin* sauce
2 tablespoons duck or plum sauce
2 tablespoons thin soy sauce
2 tablespoons Chinese rice wine or scotch
1½ tablespoons sugar
1 teaspoon sesame oil
3 cloves garlic, crushed

1 Bring 1¼ ltrs (2 pts) water to a boil in large saucepan and blanch water chestnuts 30 seconds. With Chinese mesh or long-handled slotted metal spoon, remove from water and drain in colander.

2 Cut chicken livers in 3 or 4 pieces and blanch 1 minute. Drain in colander and rinse under cold running water.

3 Pat dry and place in large bowl along with the water chestnuts.

4 Add remaining ingredients to water chestnuts and livers. Toss well. Marinate 20 minutes or until ready to cook.

5 Preheat grill.

6 On each of 8 bamboo skewers, thread a scallion piece, so that each skewer is threaded with 4 scallion sections, 3 water chestnuts, and 3 chicken livers each. Arrange skewers in heatproof pan and spoon marinade on top.

7 Place pan about 7½ cm (3 inches) from heat source and grill 5 to 7 minutes, turning once, until livers are golden but still pink in centre.

8 Serve immediately.

Shredded Chicken in Lettuce Packages

5 Chinese dried black mushrooms
250 g (8 oz) canned water chestnuts, drained
500 g (1 lb) skinless, boneless chicken breasts (about
    2 whole brests)
The marinade:
1 tablespoon thin soy sauce
1 tablespoon Chinese rice wine or Scotch
1 teaspoon sesame oil
2 tablespoons water
1½ teaspoons cornstarch
The sauce:
3 tablespoons thin soy sauce
2 tablespoons Chinese rice wine or Scotch
2 teaspoons sugar
1½ teaspoons salt
1½ teaspoons sesame oil
125 ml (4 fl oz) Chinese Chicken Stock or water
1½ teaspoons cornstarch
16 lettuce leaves, rinsed and drained
30 g (1 oz) pine nuts
1 ltr (1¾ pts) peanut, corn, or safflower oil
30 g (1 oz) thin Chinese rice noodles (maifun) or
    cellophane noodles
1 tablespoon minced scallions
1 tablespoon minced fresh ginger

1 In a small bowl, cover mushrooms with hot water and allow to soften, about 15 minutes, or until spongy. Bring 500 ml (1 pt) water to a boil in large saucepan and blanch water chestnuts 30 seconds. Drain and slice. Set aside.

2 Cut breasts in half lengthwise and then once again in half crosswise. Cut lengthwise again into matchstick-size shreds, about 5 cm (2 inches) long and 2½ mm (⅛ inch) thick.

3 Combine marinade ingredients with chicken strips in medium-size bowl, and toss to coat. Marinate 15 minutes.

4 Drain mushrooms, cut off stems, and shred caps. Stir to combine sauce ingredients in small bowl.

5 Arrange lettuce on platter and refrigerate.

6 Preheat oven to 170°C (325°F or Mark 3). Toast pine nuts on baking sheet 3 to 5 minutes, shaking pan from time to time. Remove from oven.

7 In Dutch oven, add cooking oil and heat to 200°C (400°F) on deep-fat thermometer or until smoking. Drop rice noodles into oil and deep fry several seconds until puffed and lightly golden. Turn over and deep fry a few more seconds. Remove with Chinese mesh spoon or long-handled slotted metal spoon to drain on paper towels and cool. Turn heat to low. Transfer to serving platter and with your fingers break up noodles to form a bed for chicken mixture.

8 Add chicken shreds. Stir constantly to separate the shreds and cook until they turn white. Remove with slotted metal spoon and drain on paper towels.

9 Heat large heavy skillet and add 3 tablespoons of the hot cooking oil from the Dutch oven. Add scallions and ginger, and stir-fry with wok spatula or 2 wooden spoons for 10 seconds until fragrant. Add shredded mushrooms and stir-fry another 10 seconds. Then add water chestnuts and toss lightly over high heat about 20 seconds.

10 Add sauce and stir until thickened. Add chicken shreds and pinenuts. Toss lightly over high heat to coat. Spoon chicken over the rice noodles.

11 Remove lettuce from the refrigerator. Let each person spoon a portion of chicken-and-noodles into a lettuce leaf. To eat, roll up the leaf to enclose the filling.

Michael Tong

Menu 1
(*right*)
Sautéed Scallops
Pork with Barbecue Sauce
Broccoli with Sugar Snap Peas/Rice

Michael Tong was born in Shanghai and spent his childhood first in Taiwan, then in Hong Kong, acquiring a love for both Northern-and Southern-style Chinese food. Now a New Yorker, he operates three Manhattan restaurants – an occupation that leaves him to cook for himself and his friends only as a hobby. As a result, he favours uncomplicated recipes, easily available ingredients, and an interesting variety of cooking techniques. He believes that knowing how to use many techniques is important because each contributes to the diversity of texture and flavour of the dishes.

All of Michael Tong's menus are family style, which means the dishes are particularly quick to prepare and should be served all together. And because the recipes use simple ingredients, they appeal to everyone's taste. Quick as his menus are, Mr. Tong likes to simplify things even further by preparing his meals in stages – perhaps the appetizer and soup in the morning, then the entrée at meantime. Whether you follow this advice or cook the meal all at once, you should be able to do it in twenty minutes if you gather and organize your ingredients carefully. A further piece of advice: mix your sauce ingredients first rather than add them to the dish separately. In this way, you can take a moment to adjust the sauce to your own taste, then add it to the dish with confidence.

Tender white scallops garnished with scallions and chopped parsley look appetizing against the reddish-brown pork cubes and the green vegetables. Easy to prepare, this meal is also quick to serve. Simply arrange your four plates as you finish cooking and carry them to the table.

Menu 1

Sautéed Scallops
Pork with Barbecue Sauce
Broccoli with Sugar Snap Peas/Rice

In this meal the scallops are Shanghainese and the pork in barbecue sauce is Cantonese. Though these recipes are modern adaptions, the tastes and textures are true to their traditional roots. Michael Tong believes that techniques are more crucial to any given dish than are its ingredients. For instance, if you cannot find fresh bay or sea scallops, buy a firm white-fleshed fish instead and cube it. Or, if you prefer, substitute boned chicken breasts for the pork in the second recipe: chicken works equally well, though it cooks more quickly, and gives the dish a different taste.

For best results in this menu, the sugar snap peas, or snow peas, if you prefer, should be ultrafresh – crisp and bright with the tiny peas just visible inside. To store these peas until you are ready to cook them, wrap the unwashed pods in a perforated plastic bag and refrigerate. This way they will last from four to five days. Before cooking them with the broccoli, snap off the ends and peel of the strings. If you decide to try frozen snow peas instead, cook them just long enough to get them hot. Otherwise, they will become soggy.

Broccoli, generally available fresh all year, should have a fresh green colour in the leaves and head. An ageing head of broccoli will have started to yellow. Broccoli stalks should be firm. To store a head of broccoli, wash it well, then wrap it in a plastic bag, and refrigerate.

When cooking the vegetables, watch them carefully. The broccoli, like the peas, should be crunchy and firm to the bite.

What to drink
According to Michael Tong, not all American or European wines go well with Chinese food. For this menu, he suggests an Alsatian white or a California Chenin Blanc.

Start-to-Finish Steps

1 Follow rice recipe steps 1 and 2.
2 Follow pork recipe steps 1 through 3.
3 Preheat oven to 200°C (400°F or Mark 6). Continue pork recipe steps 4 through 7.
4 Wipe out pan. Pare broccoli, removing stems, and cut florets into small pieces.
5 Follow rice recipe step 3.
6 Follow sautéed scallops recipe steps 1 through 6 and keep warm in oven.
7 Wipe out pan and cook broccoli with peas steps 1 through 4. Follow rice recipe step 4. Serve with pork, sautéed scallops, and vegetables.
8 Complete stir-fried lettuce recipe step 4, baked fish recipe step 9, rice recipe step 4, and drunken mushrooms recipe step 5. Serve.

Sautéed Scallops

500 g (1 lb) fresh bay or sea scallops
1 tablespoon cornstarch
750 ml (1 1/2 pts) vegetable oil

The sauce:
1 teaspoon salt
125 ml (4 fl oz) dry sherry
1 teaspoon cornstarch
1/4 teaspoon white pepper
2 teaspoons chopped fresh ginger
3 scallions, white part cut into rings, green part into julienne strips
2 teaspoons chopped fresh coriander
2 tablespoons sesame oil
Small tomato, cut into wedges (optional)
Coriander sprigs (optional)

1 If using sea scallops, cut them in half. Combine with 1 tablespoon cornstarch in large bowl and toss to coat.
2 Heat vegetable oil in wok or Dutch oven until almost smoking.
3 Combine sauce ingredients in small bowl.
4 Add scallops to pan, stirring to separate, and cook 3 to 4 minutes, or until they float to top of oil. Remove with Chinese mesh spoon or long-handled slotted metal spoon and drain in colander lined with paper towels. Carefully pour off oil into a container.
5 Heat wok or Dutch oven and add ginger, scallion rings, and coriander. Sauté 30 seconds, then add scallops and sauce ingredients. Cook until scallops are well coated and heated through. Swirl in sesame oil.
6 Mound scallops in centre of heated serving plate and garnish with scallion strips. Garnish plate with tomato wedges and coriander sprigs, if desired.

Pork with Barbecue Sauce

500 g (1 lb) boneless pork, or 1 Kg (2 lb) thin pork
   chops
2 egg whites
1 tablespoon cornstarch
2 teaspoons dry sherry
$^1/_4$ teaspoon salt
$^1/_4$ teaspoon white pepper

The sauce:
2 scallions, white part only, cut into julienne pieces
2 teaspoons chopped fresh ginger
2 to 3 teaspoons chopped garlic
60 ml (2 fl oz) dry sherry
2 tablespoons light soy sauce
$^1/_4$ teaspoon white pepper
2 tablespoons Oriental barbecue sauce, preferably, or
   hoisin sauce
1 teaspoon cornstarch mixed with 2 teaspoons water
1 ltr (1$^3/_4$ pts) vegetable oil
2 tablespoons sesame oil

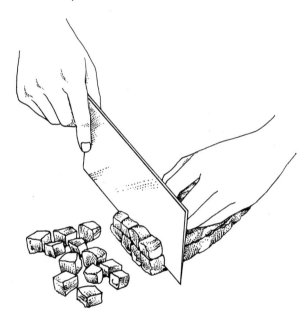

1 Cut pork into 1 cm ($^1/_2$ inch) cubes. If using pork
   chops, remove meat and discard bones.
2 Lightly beat egg whites in large bowl. Add cubed
   pork, tossing to coat well. Stir together cornstarch,
   sherry, salt, and pepper in small bowl. Add to pork
   and with your fingers toss to combine.
3 With a fork, combine sauce ingredients in small
   bowl.
4 Heat vegetable oil in wok or Dutch oven until almost
   smoking (about 180°C (350°F) on deep-fat
   thermometer).
5 Add pork cubes a few at a time to prevent sticking.
   Cook until golden brown, about 3 minutes. Remove

with Chinese mesh spoon or long-handled slotted
metal spoon to drain in metal colander. Repeat until
all the meat is cooked. If using wok, pour off oil into
a container.
6 Heat wok or large heavy skillet and add sauce and
   drained pork. Cook until thickened and blended.
   Swirl in sesame oil.
7 Pour pork and sauce onto heated serving plate and
   keep warm in preheated slow oven.

Broccoli with Sugar Snap Peas

3 tablespoons vegetable oil
1 large bunch broccoli, stems removed and florets cut
   into small pieces
250 g (8 oz) sugar snap or snow peas (about 30)
60 ml (2 fl oz) Chinese Chicken stock
2 tablespoons dry sherry
$^1/_4$ teaspoon salt
$^1/_2$ teaspoon sugar
1 tablespoon cornstarch mixed with 1 tablespoon
   water
$^1/_2$ teaspoon sesame oil

1 In wok or large heavy skillet, heat oil until almost
   smoking.
2 Add broccoli and peas. Stir fry 30 seconds.
3 Add stock, sherry, salt, and sugar. Cook at a boil 2
   minutes.
4 Add cornstarch mixture and sesame oil. Toss 30
   seconds until well coated. Serve.

Rice

300 g (10 oz) long-grain rice
625 ml (1$^1/_4$ pts) water

1 Wash rice by rubbing it between your hands in
   several changes of water to remove any excess
   starch.
2 Combine rice and water in 1$^1/_2$ ltr (3 pt) saucepan.
   Bring to a boil over high heat. Continue to boil rice,
   uncovered, about 5 minutes, until virtually all
   visible water has evaporated, leaving bubbles and
   air holes on surface of rice.
3 Cover pan and simmer over very low heat 18 or 20
   minutes.
4 Uncover and stir well to fluff rice before serving.

Menu 2

Egg Drop Soup with Tomato
Orange Beef
Stir-Fried Bok Choy/Rice

This meal features egg drop soup, thick with threads of yolk that form when you stir beaten eggs into the hot chicken broth. This version includes chopped fresh tomatoes.

Bok choy, a variety of Chinese cabbage, has white fleshy stems and dark green leaves. When cooked, it is both tender and sweet. If it is not available, you may substitute such lettuces as Cos or leaf lettuce.

What to drink

This is an excellent combination of flavours to show off a Moselle wine: choose a Wehlener or an Erdener.

Start-to-Finish Steps

1 Follow orange beef recipe steps 1 through 4.
2 Prepare bok choy, step 1.
3 Preheat oven to 200°C (400°F or Mark 6). Cook orange beef, steps 5 through 10.
4 Follow egg drop soup recipe steps 1 and 2.
5 Wipe out pan. Follow bok choy recipe steps 2 and 3.
6 Follow egg drop soup recipe steps 3 through 5, bok choy recipe step 4, and serve with orange beef.

Egg Drop Soup with Tomato

1 large tomato
1 ltr (1^3/$_4$ pts) Chinese Chicken Stock
^{1}/$_4$ teaspoon salt
2 teaspoons dry sherry
3 tablespoons cornstarch blended with 3 tablespoons water
2 eggs, lightly beaten
1 teaspoon sesame oil

1 Bring 250 ml (8 fl oz) water to a boil in medium-size saucepan and blanch tomato 1 minute. Remove with slotted metal spoon. Cool slightly and chop. You should have about 175 ml (6 fl oz).
2 Put tomato and stock in same saucepan and bring to a boil. Cook over high heat 2 minutes.
3 Stir in salt, sherry, and cornstarch mixture, and cook 1 minute.
4 Slowly add beaten eggs in a stream, stirring with chopsticks or a wooden spoon. Swirl in sesame oil.
5 Pour into soup tureen or individual bowls.

Orange Beef

500 g (1 lb) flank steak
2 egg whites
3 tablespoons cornstarch
125 ml (4 fl oz) dry sherry
2 tablespoons light soy sauce
60 g (2 oz) sugar
4 tablespoons white vinegar
^{1}/$_4$ teaspoon white pepper
750 ml (1^1/$_2$ pts) vegetable oil
1 red bell pepper
4 scallions, white part only
1 small yellow squash
3 tablespoons dried orange peel, or 2 tablespoons fresh grated orange rind
1 tablespoon sesame oil

1 Using cleaver or chef's knife, slice flank steak on diagonal into 5 mm (^{1}/$_4$ inch) slices. Stack slices and cut into 5 mm (^{1}/$_4$ inch) strips.
2 Lightly beat egg whites in medium-size bowl and add flank steak. With your fingers mix well.

Every dish in this family-style meal features festive colour, so you need no garnish. Serving pieces are simple, too.

3 Sprinkle in 2 tablespoons of the cornstarch and mix well.
4 Combine remaining cornstarch and next five ingredients in small bowl, stirring to dissolve cornstarch.
5 Heat oil in wok or Dutch oven until almost smoking.
6 Core and seed pepper, and cut into diagonal chunks.
7 Cut scallions lengthwise into thin slices.
8 Cut squash into quarters, then into matchstick-size pieces.
9 When oil is almost smoking, carefully add flank steak piece by piece using Chinese mesh spoon or slotted metal spoon, stirring so that the pieces do not stick together. Toss them in oil until they turn dark golden brown, about 1 minute. Add red pepper and cook 1 minute. Remove meat and pepper with the spoon and drain in colander. If using wok, carefully pour off oil into a container.
10 Heat wok or large deep skillet and add sesame oil, scallions, squash, and orange peel. Wait 30 seconds, then add meat, peppers, and sauce. Cook, tossing and stirring, until thickened. Transfer food to heated serving platter and keep warm in slow oven.

Stir-Fried Bok Choy

1 head bok choy (about 750 g–1Kg (1¹/₂–2 lb))
3 tablespoon vegetable oil
¹/₂ tablespoon chopped fresh ginger
125 ml (4 fl oz) Chinese Chicken stock
¹/₂ teaspoon salt
¹/₂ teaspoon sugar
2 tablespoons dry sherry
1 tablespoons cornstarch blended with 1 teaspoon
   water

1 Chop off tops of bok choy leaves and discard. cut remaining leaves in half and then into 3¹/₂ cm (1¹/₂ inch) pieces. Rinse and pat dry with paper towels.
2 Heat wok or skillet and vegetable oil. When almost smoking, add ginger and bok choy. Stir-fry 30 seconds.
3 Add stock, salt, sugar, and sherry. Cook 2 minutes.
4 Stir cornstarch mixture again and to pan. Cook, stirring just until thickened, about 30 seconds.

Bean Curd Salad with Peanuts
Steamed Sea Bass with Black Bean Sauce
Chicken, Szechwan Style/Rice

Bean curd salad and whole steamed fish look especially attractive if you arrange them on beds of fresh green lettuce.

This meal also offers some regional contrasts: the steamed sea bass is typically Cantonese, and the bean curd salad with peanuts and the chicken are spicy Szechwan-style dishes. Cooks in the western provinces frequently use nuts to flavour their dishes, their favourites being almonds, cashews, walnuts, and peanuts. For this particular recipe, use regular unsalted peanuts if the dried variety are not available. The salad is excellent for other meals as well, particularly picnics.

What to drink
An Italian Pinot Grigio or Verdicchio or a French Muscadet will all provide dryness, fruit, and acidity to complement the meal.

Start-to-Finish Steps
1 For steamed sea bass recipe, slice and cut ginger into thin strips and cut white part of scallions into thin strips.
2 Prepare steamed sea bass, steps 1 through 3.
3 While fish is steaming, follow rice recipe steps 1 and 2.
4 Chop scallions and coriander for bean curd salad, and ginger, scallions, garlic, and red bell pepper for Szechwan chicken.
5 Follow Szechwan chicken recipe steps 1 through 7.
6 Follow rice recipe step 3.
7 Make bean curd salad steps 1 through 3.
8 Follow rice recipe step 4, Szechwan chicken recipe step 8, and steam sea bass step 4. Serve.

Bean curd Salad with Peanuts

4 large squares fresh firm bean curd
1 teaspoon chopped fresh ginger
2 tablespoons chopped scallion, white part only
1 1/2 teaspoons chopped fresh coriander
1 teaspoon sesame chili oil (optional)
1 tablespoon dry sherry
1 tablespoon light soy sauce
2 teaspoons sesame oil
1/2 teaspoon salt
1/2 teaspoon sugar
Curly lettuce and quartered tomatoes (optional)
3 tablespoons dry roasted peanuts for garnish
   (optional)

1 Cut bean curd squares into 5 mm (1/4 inch) cubes and place in medium-size bowl.

50

2 Sprinkle remaining ingredients except peanuts over bean curd and with your fingers toss lightly to blend.

3 Mound salad on serving plate with lettuce and tomato, and sprinkle with peanuts for garnish, if desired.

Steamed Sea Bass with Black Bean Sauce

1 Kg (2 lb) fresh whole sea bass, boned and butterflied, or 750 g (1¹/₂ lb) fillets
7 small slices fresh ginger, cut into thin strips
4 scallions, white part only, cut into thin strips
1 tablespoon Chinese fermented black beans
¹/₂ teaspoon salt
2 tablespoons dry sherry
1 teaspoon white pepper
1 tablespoon vegetable oil
Curly lettuce for garnish (optional)

1 Bring 1 cm (¹/₂ inch) water to a boil in stockpot or large sauté pan.

2 Make a diagonal slit on bith sides of whole fish or in each fillet and wash fish under cold running water to remove any debris and blood. Place fish cut side up on an oval plate slightly smaller than steaming vessel.

3 Combine remaining ingredients, except lettuce, in small bowl and sprinkle over fish. Set plate on metal trivet in pan. Cover and steam fish 20 minutes, or until fish flakes easily and is opaque. Check water level occasionally.

4 To serve, place plate in which fish was steamed directly onto another larger platter. Garnish with lettuce, if desired.

Chicken, Szechwan Style

1 whole skinless, boneless chicken breast (about 500 g (1 lb))
2 egg whites
2 tablespoons cornstarch plus 1 teaspoon cornstarch mixed with 2 teaspoons water

The sauce:
¹/₂ teaspoon white pepper
2 tablespoons light soy sauce
60 ml (2 fl oz) dry sherry
1 teaspoon sugar
2 tablespoons sesame oil
750 ml (1¹/₂ pts) vegetable oil
2 teaspoons chopped fresh ginger

2 scallions, white part only, sliced into thin rings
1 teaspoon chopped garlic
1 red bell pepper, cut into 5 mm (¹/₄ inch) strips and then into diagonal pieces

1 Hold cleaver or chef's knife parallel to work surface and cut chicken breast in half, making thin pieces. Cut each piece into 2¹/₂ cm (1 inch) dice.

2 Lightly beat egg whites in large bowl. Add chicken and mix well. Add 2 tablespoons cornstarch and mix well so that chicken pieces are evenly coated.

3 Combine sauce ingredients plus cornstarch mixture in small bowl.

4 Heat oil in wok or Dutch oven over medium-high heat until almost smoking.

5 Place ginger, scallions, and garlic in small bowl.

6 When oil is almost smoking, gently add chicken pieces, a few at a time, and stir so that they do not stick together. Toss the chicken in the oil about 2 minutes. Add red pepper and stir with metal wok spatula 30 seconds.

7 Carefully pour chicken and peppers into metal colander set over large bowl to catch the oil.

8 Reheat pan and add ginger, garlic, and scallions. Wait 1 second, then add chicken and sauce ingredients. Toss to coat chicken and combine flavours. Remove to heated serving platter.

Rice

300 g (10 oz) long-grain rice
625 ml (1¹/₄ pts) water

1 Wash rice by rubbing it between your hands in several changes of water to remove any excess starch.

2 Combine rice and water in 1¹/₂ ltr (3 pt) saucepan. Bring to a boil over high heat. Continue to boil rice, uncovered, about 5 minutes, until virtually all visible water has evaporated, leaving bubbles and air holes on surface of rice.

3 Cover pan and simmer over very low heat 18 or 20 minutes.

4 Uncover and stir well to fluff rice before serving.

Jeri Sipe

Menu 1
(*right*)
Sweet and Sour Cucumber Salad
Quick Barbecued Pork
Fish Steaks with Hot Sauce
Rice

The thrifty Chinese waste nothing edible. Ingenious and practical, they have recipes for even the most humble ingredients. Their skilled cooks can extend small portions of food to feed many and still retain peak flavour and aroma. Jeri Sipe, an Oregon-based cooking teacher who was born and raised in Taiwan, shows her students how to practise this kitchen economy. She stresses the use of fresh ingredients, never overcooked, but believes that cooks can concoct a fine Chinese meal with leftovers if the food was fresh and of high quality to begin with.

Before coming to the United states, Jeri Sipe cooked professionally in Taiwan for many years, learning traditional recipes and techniques. She interprets them in these three menus, all of which have their roots in northern Chinese and Taiwanese styles – that is, they are imaginative blendings of both the sweet and the spicy. Menus 1 and 3 particularly demonstrate this blending: tangy meats are contrasted with the cool, sweet taste of vegetables. Like any accomplished Chinese cook, Jeri Sipe strives to balance tastes and to avoid serving a meal that completely overwhelms the palate. Menu 3 features a typical Taiwanese speciality – vegetable balls. Served with a sweet and sour sauce, they make a delicious appetizer.

To set the table for this meal, you need serving platters for the main courses and small side dishes to hold the toasted sesame seeds, hot pepper sauce, and mustard sauce. Pass the sauces, or provide a bowl of each sauce for each guest. To unify your setting, use colour-coordinated dishes that have contrasting shapes.

This recipe calls for pork shoulder, an economical cut, which you slice for barbecuing. If you wish, substitute a leaner cut – boneless loin, for example. It will cost more but will be considerably lower in fat, and you will have fewer scraps to throw away.

One of the subtle tastes in the marinade for the pork is Chinese five-spice, which Chinese cooks use in every form of regional cuisine. It should be part of your regular Chinese pantry, and you can blend it at home if you like. Simply combine roughly equal portions of cinnamon sticks, cloves, brown Szechwan peppercorns, fennel, and star anise in a blender, and grind them fine.

Serve the pork with two simple dipping sauces, as directed in the recipe. The first – ketchup, hot pepper sauce, and Worcestershire – can be as mild or as hot as you like, depending on the amount of hot pepper sauce you add, and the mustard sauce is very hot. The toasted sesame seeds provide another flavourful, crunchy dip for the pork.

Fresh swordfish, if you can find it, is a dry, white, meaty fish and the best choice for this recipe. If you cannot get it or prefer something less expensive, halibut or any other thick, boneless fish steak will also work well. Be sure to rinse the fish steaks and pat them dry with paper towels before beginning the recipe.

The piquant sauce served with the fish provides another spicy yet contrasting flavour. The recipe calls for two fresh or dried hot red chili peppers sold in jars at most supermarkets, although they are not as strong or as flavourful. One teaspoon is equal to one small dried red chili.

The sweet and sour cucumber is the cooling taste contrast for the whole meal. Start with cold cucumbers and then return them to the refrigerator after you have set them to marinate.

What to drink
The variety of flavours here will fight most wines, so opt for cold beer, ale, or tea.

Start-to-Finish Steps
1 Follow rice recipe steps 1 and 2.
2 Follow sweet and sour cucumber recipe step 1.
3 Follow barbecued pork recipe steps 1 and 2.
4 Follow fish steaks recipe steps 1 through 5.
5 Follow sweet and sour cucumber recipe step 2.

6 Preheat oven to 200°C (400°F or Mark 6) and complete barbecued pork recipe, steps 3 through 7.
7 Follow rice recipe step 3.
8 Follow sweet and sour cucumber recipe step 3.
9 Wipe out pan and cook fish steaks, steps 6 through 11. Follow barbecued pork recipe step 8, rice recipe step 4, and bring everything to the table.

Sweet and Sour Cucumber Salad

2 cucumbers
1 teaspoon salt
3 teaspoons vinegar
3 tablespoons suger

1 Peel cucumbers and slice in half lengthwise. Scoop out seeds and slice halves crosswise into 2$\frac{1}{2}$ mm ($\frac{1}{8}$ inch) pieces. Place them in colander and mix well with salt. Let stand 15 minutes.
2 Drain off salty water. Put cucumbers in small bowl and add vinegar and sugar. Let stand 10 minutes.
3 Before serving, squeeze and drain sweet and sour juice from cucumber slices. Place cucumbers in serving bowl.

Quick Barbecued Pork

500 g (1 lb) pork shoulder

The marinade:
1 tablespoon *hoisin* sauce
Pinch Chinese five-spice
1 tablespoon light soy sauce
1$\frac{1}{2}$ tablespoons ginger wine or dry sherry
2 teaspoons honey
$\frac{1}{2}$ teaspoon sesame oil
1$\frac{1}{2}$ tablespoons potato starch, preferably, or
  cornstarch
3 tablespoons ketchup
4 drops hot pepper sauce
$\frac{1}{4}$ teaspoon Worcestershire sauce
1 tablespoon hot mustard powder
2 tablespoons warm water
2 tablespoons toasted sesame seeds
1 ltr (1$\frac{3}{4}$ pts) peanut or vegetable oil

1 Slice pork horizontally into 1 cm ($\frac{1}{2}$ inch) slices,
   then cut into strips about 7$\frac{1}{2}$ cm (3 inches) long and
   1 cm ($\frac{1}{2}$ inch) wide.
2 Combine marinade ingredients in medium-size bowl
   and add pork. Mix thoroughly and let stand 10
   minutes or longer.
3 Mix ketchup, hot pepper sauce, and Worcestershire
   in small serving bowl.
4 In another small bowl, stir mustard powder and
   water until a thick paste is formed. Cover with plastic
   wrap.
5 Put sesame seeds in third small serving bowl.
6 Heat cooking oil in wok or Dutch oven to 190°C
   (375°F) on deep-fat thermometer. Carefully add
   pork and any of the marinade left in bowl, and cook
   about 2 minutes. Use metal wok or spatula or slotted
   metal spoon to stir pork and keep it from sticking
   together.
7 Remove pork from oil with Chinese mesh spoon or
   long-handled slotted metal spoon and drain well.
   Place on serving platter and keep warm in oven.
8 When ready to serve, garnish with some sesame
   seeds, if desired, and serve with the hot sauce,
   mustard, and sesame seeds as dips.

Fish Steaks with Hot Sauce

2 swordfish or halibut steaks (about 300 g (10 oz)
    each), 2$\frac{1}{2}$ cm (1 inch) thick
125 ml (4 fl oz) beef or Chinese Chicken Stock
2 teaspoons oyster sauce
1$\frac{1}{4}$ teaspoons cornstarch
1 teaspoon chili paste

1 teaspoon sesame oil
4 scallions
3 slices fresh ginger
2 fresh or dried hot red peppers
1 teaspoon brown sugar
1 tablespoon mushroom soy sauce or light soy sauce
2 tablespoons ginger wine or dry sherry
60 ml (2 fl oz) peanut or vegetable oil

1 Rinse fish under cold running water and pat dry.
2 Combine stock, oyster sauce, cornstarch, chilli paste,
   and sesame oil in small saucepan. Stir well and set
   aside.
3 Cut white portion of scallions into 5 cm (2 inch)
   pieces. Chop enough of green portion to make 1
   tablespoon. Set aside seperately.
4 Combine ginger, white scallion pieces, and hot red
   peppers.
5 In small bowl, combine brown sugar, mushroom
   soy sauce, and ginger wine or dry sherry. Set aside.
6 Heat oil in wok or heavy skillet until hot. Place fish
   in pan and brown about 3 minutes. As fish steaks are
   browning, sprinkle ginger, red pepper, and white
   part of scallions over them.
7 Turn fish and fry other side 3 minutes.
8 Remove pan from heat and carefully pour off all but
   1 tablespoon of the oil and return pan to stove.
   Continue to brown fish steaks and sprinkle over
   them the sugar and soy sauce mixtuer. Cook until
   fish flakes when gently touched with a fork.
9 Meanwhile, over medium-high heat, bring oyster
   sauce mixture to a boil, stirring constantly. Continue
   to cook until sauce just begins to thicken.
10 Quickly pour sauce over fish and let simmer about
   3 minutes.
11 Remove fish with sauce to serving plate. Garnish
   with the tablespoon of chopped scallions greens.

Rice

300 g (10 oz) long-grain rice
625 ml (1$\frac{1}{4}$ pts) water

1 Wash rice by rubbing it between your hands in
   several changes of water to remove any excess
   starch.
2 Combine rice and water in 1$\frac{1}{2}$ ltr (3 pt) saucepan.
   Bring to a boil over high heat. Continue to boil rice,
   uncovered, about 5 minutes, until virtually all
   visible water has evaporated, leaving bubbles and
   air holes on surface of rice.
3 Cover pan and simmer over very low heat 18 or 20
   minutes.
4 Uncover and stir well to fluff rice before serving.

<table>
<tr>
<td>

Menu

2

</td>
<td>

Spicy Fried Calf's Liver
Mountain Snow White Chicken/Rice

</td>
</tr>
</table>

Besides being rich in texture, colour, and flavour, this meal is nutritionaly rich as well: it contains calf's liver, chicken, rice, and several vegetables. Select liver that is pale and odourless, and before cooking it, remove membranes to prevent the liver from curling up when cooked.

Your shopping list for this menu includes two essential Chinese ingredients – oyster sauce and chili paste. Oyster sauce is a typical Cantonese condiment. It has a rich, salty, rather strong oyster taste and is used frequently to flavour stir-fries and as a condiment at the table. After opening, oyster sauce should be stored in the refrigerator, where it will last indefinitely. Chili paste, sold in jars, is made from fresh ground red chilies, garlic, and other spices. Because this paste is very hot, use it sparingly in cooking or serve it as a condiment. This, too, should be stored in the refrigerator. There are no substitutes for either of these.

Mushroom soy sauce, on the other hand, is good to have as an option. Delicately flavoured with mushrooms and saltier than standard light soy sauces, mushroom soy sauce tastes delicious in stir-fries. Unfortunately it is difficult to find, but you wil not harm the recipe if you use regular soy sauce instead.

Ginger wine, a flavouring ingredient for the calf's liver marinade, is easily made by soaking four to five ounces of peeled, minced fresh ginger in Chinese rice wine. In a few days, the wine is ready to use. The wine lasts indefinately when stored in the refrigerator.

When sugar snap peas are not in season, use snow peas, which are usually in the market year round. Straw mushrooms, which have a silken texture and a very delicate taste, are often used in stir-fried dishes and soups. If you have access to a Chinese produce market, ask for fresh straw mushrooms, which are small and brown, and take their name from the straw on which they grow. Fresh ones will keep three to four days in the refrigerator, and the canned ones will keep for a week after opening, provided you store them in a covered container.

Savoy white chicken with snow pieces, rich brown calf's liver garnished with radishes, combined with rice and tea, satisfy big appetites. Provide your guests with chopsticks for eating this elegant meal.

What to drink

Here again the flavours of the dishes are not really compatible with wine, so serve beer, ale, or tea.

Start-to-Finish Steps

1 Follow rice (see page 9) recipe steps 1 and 2.
2 Follow fried calf's liver recipe step 1. Lightly beat egg white for chicken and follow snow white chicken recipe steps 1 and 2.
3 Preheat oven to 200°C (400°F or Mark 6).
4 Follow fried calf's liver recipe steps 2 through 5.
5 Wipe out wok. Follow rice recipe step 3.
6 Complete snow white chicken dish, steps 3 through 10, fried calf's liver recipe step 6, and rice recipe step 4. Serve.

Spicy Fried Calf's Liver

500 g (1 lb) calf's liver
1 teaspoon mushroom soy sauce or light soy sauce
1 tablespoon ginger wine, preferably, or dry sherry
$1/8$ teaspoon black pepper

The sauce:
1 scallion, including top, thinly sliced
$1/2$ teaspoon sesame oil
$1/4$ teaspoon sugar
60 ml (2 fl oz) light soy sauce
1 teaspoon oyster sauce
3 cloves garlic, minced
2 teaspoons wine vinegar
$1/2$ teaspoon chili paste
1 ltr ($1^3/4$ pts) peanut or vegetable oil
60 g (2 oz) cornstarch

1 Cut liver into small serving pieces. Rinse, pat dry with paper towels, and place in medium-size bowl. Add mushroom or light soy sauce, ginger wine, and black pepper. Mix thoroughly. Let stand 10 minutes longer.
2 In small bowl, stir to combine sauce ingredients.
3 Heat oil in wok or Dutch oven or over medium-high heat to 190°C (375°F) on deep-fat thermometer. Put cornstarch on small plate.
4 Dust marinated liver with cornstarch, making sure that all pieces are evenly but lightly coated.
5 When oil is very hot, carefully add half the liver pieces and cook about 1 to 2 minutes. remove from oil with Chinese mesh spoon or long-handled slotted metal spoon and place on heatproof serving platter lined with paper towels to drain. Keep warm in preheated slow oven while you cook remaining half.
6 When ready to serve, pour sauce over liver and garnish with radishes.

Mountain Snow White Chicken

750 g ($1^1/2$ lb) skinless, boneless chicken breasts (about 2 whole breasts)

The marinade:
1 tablespoon cornstarch
$1/4$ teaspoon baking soda
1 tablespoon vegetable oil
1 tablespoon dry white wine
1 egg white, lightly beaten
Pinch salt

The sauce:
125 ml (4 fl oz) Chinese Chicken Stock
1 tablespoon ginger wine, preferably, or dry sherry
1 teaspoon sesame oil
$1^1/2$ teaspoons cornstarch
12 snow peas, preferably, or sugar snap
16 straw mushrooms
1 tablespoon peanut or vegetable oil
$1/2$ teaspoon minced ginger
$1/2$ teaspoon minced garlic
1 tablespoon minced onion

1 Slice chicken into pieces about $7^1/2$ cm (3 inches) long, $2^1/2$ cm (1 inch) wide, and 5 mm ($1/4$ inch) thick, or into long slices.
2 Combine marinade ingredients in medium-size mixing bowl. Add chicken and mix thoroughly to coat well. Let stand 10 minutes longer.
3 Bring $2^1/2$ ltrs (4 pts) water to a boil in large saucepan.
4 Combine sauce ingredients in small bowl, stirring to dissolve cornstarch.
5 Rinse peas and pull off strings. Set aside in small bowl with straw mushrooms.
6 Add marinated chicken to the boiling water and cook, stirring, until chicken begins to turn white, about 1 minute. Pour chicken into colander and drain well.
7 Heat cooking oil in wok or large, heavy skillet. When oil is hot, add ginger, garlic, and onion, and using 40 cm (16 inch) chopsticks or wooden spoon, and stir-fry a few seconds.
8 Add straw mushrooms and peas, and stir-fry 30 seconds.
9 Stir sauce once more and add to pan. Add blanched chicken and bring sauce to a boil, stirring constantly until sauce begins to thicken.
10 Remove from heat and place chicken on heated serving plate.

Vegetable Balls with Sweet and Sour Sauce
Spicy Lamb with Tree Ear Mushrooms
Sautéed Shrimp with Cucumbers/Rice

An attractive way to present this meal in individual unmatched serving pieces that underline the contrasting colours of the plate orange shrimp, the golden vegetable balls, and the brown spicy lamb.

As a child, Jeri Sipe helped prepare this recipe for vegetable balls as part of an annual family feast. She recalls picking the vegetables – cabbage, onions, carrots and water chestnuts – in the fields, then making the the vegetable balls with her mother. The sweet and sour dipping sauce that accompanies them here is thought to have originated in Canton.

Lamb, a Mongolian favorite, has always been more popular in Northern than in Southern China, but centuries ago almost all Chinese considered lamb unfit for civilized people. The reason; its strong aroma. Although attitudes have changed, lamb is still not readily available in Southern China. Whenever this meat is used, regardless of the region, Chinese cooks generally slice or shred it and camouflage it with strong ingredients. For this recipe, Jeri Sipe calls for cutting a boned lamb shoulder into pieces that are then marinated in ginger wine, mushroom soy sauce, cinnamon, and sesame oil. The dried tree ear mushrooms that accompany the lamb look like crumpled scorched paper, but soaking restores them to their original size. For appearance as for flavour, there are no direct Western mushroom equivalents, but you could use a dried European mushroom.

What to drink
A well-chilled soave or similar dry, fruity wine, or a California Semillon or Emerald Riesling can accompany these dishes.

Start-to-Finish Steps
1 Follow spicy lamb recipe steps 1 through 3.
2 Follow rice recipe steps 1 and 2.
3 Follow vegetable balls recipe steps 1 and 2.
4 Follow sautéed shrimp recipe steps 1 through 6.
5 Preheat oven to 200°C (400°F or Mark 6). Follow spicy lamb step 4 through 11.
6 Wipe out pan. Follow vegetable balls recipe steps 3 through 5 and rice recipe step 3.
7 Wipe out pan very well. Complete sautéed shrimp recipe, steps 7 and 8.
8 Present dipping sauces for vegetable balls, step 6, follow rice recipe, step 4, and serve the hot food immediately. Be sure to remove hot red peppers from lamb dish before serving.

Vegetable Balls with Sweet and Sour Sauce

1 small onion (about 125 g (4 oz))
1/4 head cabbage, coarsely chopped
1/2 carrot, trimmed and peeled
16 to 26 water chestnuts

1 teaspoon peanut or vegetable oil
30 g (1 oz) flour
1 tablespoon plus 2 teaspoons cornstarch
1 egg, beaten
1/4 teaspoon baking soda
1/2 teaspoon baking powder
Black pepper
2 tablespoons plus 1/2 teaspoon sugar
1/4 teaspoon salt
1 ltr (1 3/4 pts) peanut or vegetable oil
125 ml (4 fl oz) water
2 tablespoons white or Chinese dark vinegar
1 1/2 tablespoons catsup

1 Mince onion, cabbage, carrot, and water chestnuts in food processor fitted with steel blade or with sharp knife. Combine vegetables, 1 teaspoon oil, flour, and 1 teaspoon cornstarch in large mixing bowl. Add half the beaten egg and combine thoroughly.
2 Add baking soda, baking powder, dash of black pepper, 2 teaspoons sugar, and salt. Mix thoroughly.
3 Heat oil in wok or large heavy skillet to 190°C (375°F) on deep-fat thermometer.
4 For the sauce, dissolve remaining cornstarch in the water in small saucepan and add vinegar, remaining sugar, and catsup. Bring sauce to a boil and cook until it begins to thicken. Turn off heat. Cover pan; set aside.
5 Shape vegetable mixture into small patties or, using a small spoon dipped in water, form walnut-size balls. Gently drop them into the hot oil until there is 1 layer. Fry until golden brown on all sides. Remove with Chinese mesh spoon or long-handled slotted metal spoon and drain on heatproof plate lined with paper towels. Repeat until all the vegetable balls have been cooked. Keep warm in preheated slow oven.
6 Place sweet and sour sauce in bowl and serve as a dip for the vegetable balls.

Spicy Lamb with Tree Ear Mushrooms

20 g (3/4 oz) dried tree ear mushrooms (about 10)

The marinade:
1 tablespoon ginger wine or dry sherry
1 tablespoon mushroom soy sauce, preferably, or light soy sauce
1/4 teaspoon baking soda
Dash of cinnamon
1 1/2 teaspoons sesame oil
1 pound boneless lamb shoulder

The sauce:
1 tablespoon oyster sauce
1 teaspoon cornstarch
1/2 teaspoon Worcestershire sauce
60 ml (2 fl oz) beef broth or water
3 scallions, including tops, cut in 5 cm (2 inch) lengths
4 hot red peppers
1 teaspoon minced garlic
2 teaspoons minced fresh ginger
1 small red bell pepper, cored, seeded, and sliced thin
2 tablespoons peanut or vegetable oil

1   In small bowl, cover mushrooms with boiling water and allow to soak about 15 to 20 minutes.
2   Combine marinade ingredients in large mixing bowl.
3   Slice lamb horizontally into 2 1/2 mm (1/8 inch) thick pieces, and then cut into 7 1/2 cm (3 inch) squares. Add lamb to marinade and mix thoroughly.
4   Combine sauce ingredients in small bowl. Stir well to dissolve cornstarch.
5   Rinse tree ears under running water. Cut off and discard stems. Cut tree ears into 5 mm (1/4 inch) strips.
6   Place white parts of scallions in small bowl with hot red peppers, garlic, and ginger. Add cut green tops to the tree ears.
7   Heat wok or skillet. Add oil and heat until very hot. Add ginger and scallion mixture. Stir-fry about 5 seconds.
8   Add lamb and marinade and stir constantly 1 minute.
9   Add tree ears, scallion greens, and red bell pepper strips. Stir fry until tree ears are heated through.
10 Stir sauce once more and add to pan. Mix thoroughly and cook, stirring, until sauce begins to thicken.
11 Pour contents into heated serving dish and keep warm in oven. Remove the hot red peppers before serving.

Sautéed Shrimp with Cucumbers

350 g (12 oz) medium-size fresh shrimp
1/8 teaspoon baking soda
1 tablespoon cornstarch
Pinch of salt

The sauce:
125 ml (4 fl oz) Chinese Chicken Stock or fish broth
1 teaspoon cornstarch
2 teaspoons oyster sauce
3/4 teaspoon sesame oil
1 medium-size cucumber
2 tablespoons peanut or vegetable oil
1/2 small onion, sliced thin
3 1 1/2 cm (3/4 inch) square slices fresh ginger
1/4 teaspoon cayenne pepper
1/2 carrot, peeled and sliced thin
2 tablespoons dry white wine

1   Shell and devein shrimp by cutting a slit along backs. Rinse under cold running water and pat dry with paper towels.
2   Combine baking soda, cornstarch, and salt in medium-size bowl and add shrimp, tossing to mix well.
3   Bring 1 1/4 ltrs (2 pts) water to a boil in medium-size saucepan for blanching shrimp.
4   Combine sauce ingredients in small bowl.
5   Peel cucumber and slice it in half lengthwise. Scoop out seeds and cut cucumber crosswise into 5 mm (1/4 inch) slices.
6   Blanch shrimp 20 seconds and drain in colander.
7   Heat peanut oil in wok or skillet over medium heat. Add onion, ginger, and Cayenne pepper, and stir-fry 5 seconds. Add cucumber and carrot slices and stir-fry 20 seconds. Add wine and shrimp, and stir constantly 1 minute.
8   Stir sauce once more and pour over shrimp. Cook, stirring constantly, until sauce is heated through. Pour shrimp and sauce onto heated serving plate.

Meet the Cooks

Jean Yueh

Lecturer, TV guest chef and food consultant Jean Yueh has taught Chinese cooking for more than fifteen years. Her books include *The Great Tastes of Chinese Cooking* and *Dim Sum and Chinese One-Dish Meals*.

Barbara Tropp

Barbara Tropp is a retired scholar turned Chinese cook. After studying Chinese art and literature at Princeton University, she lived for two years in Taiwan, where she learned to appreciate Chinese cooking. She is the author of the highly acclaimed *The Modern Art of Chinese Cooking*.

Audrey and Calvin Lee

The late Calvin Lee came from a long line of professional chefs, starting his cooking career at the age of 17 in his family's New York restaurant. Audrey Lee learned Chinese cookery from her husband. Together they wrote several cookery books, including *The Gourmet Chinese Regional Cookbook*, *Chinese Cooking for American Kitchens* and *Chinatown, USA*.

Nina Simonds

Nina Simonds, author of *Classic Chinese Cuisine*, has translated and edited several other books, including *Chinese Cuisine* and *Chinese Snacks*. She learned to cook in Taiwan under the direction of Chinese master chef Huang Su-Huei. She also studied for a year at La Varenne Ecole de Cuisine in Paris and is the holder of a Grande Diplome in classic French cuisine.

Michael Tong

A Shanghai native brought up in Taiwan and Hong Kong, Michael Tong is a restauranteur whose personal hobby is cooking. He moved to the United States in 1963 and owns and directs the three Shun Lee restaurants in Manhattan.

Jeri Sipe

Jeri Sipe was born in Taiwan and learned to cook before she learned to read. By the age of nine, she was working as a cook in a wealthy household, and by adulthood, she had become a full-fledged, professional. She now lives in Oregon, USA.

A Wealth of Herbs

Increasingly, herbs are arriving in the markets fresh; the proliferation of health stores and other specialist shops has widened choice, and many cooks with gardens have taken to raising their own. Recent ethnic influences have called attention to once seemingly esoteric herbs. Coriander, for one, is at last gaining deserved popularity in Europe, although cooks in Asia and the Middle East have been using it for centuries.

Anyone wishing to dry fresh herbs can tie them loosely in a bundle and hang them upside down in a cool, dark, well-ventilated place for several weeks. When the leaves are completely dried, strip them from the stems and store them in an airtight container.

Two swifter methods of preserving herbs make use of the microwave oven and the freezer. To microwave herbs, place five or six sprigs at a time between paper towels and microwave them on high for 1 to 3 minutes until the leaves are brittle. Store the leaves loosely in airtight jars.

To freeze herbs, rinse the sprigs and pat them dry. Strip the leaves off the stems and put them into a heavy-duty plastic bag. Gently flatten the bag to force out the air, seal the bag tightly, and place it in your freezer. Use the leaves as the need arises.

Basil (also called sweet basil): This fragrant herb, with its underlying flavour of anise and hint of clove, goes particularly well with tomato.

Chervil: The small, lacy leaves of this herb have a taste akin to parsley with a touch of anise. It is good in salads and salad dressings. Chervil is popular in France, where it is often an ingredient in herb mixtures, including *fines herbes*. When used in cooking, chervil should be added at the end, lest its subtle flavour be lost.

Chives: The smallest of the onions, chives grow in grassy clumps. When finely cut, the hollow leaves contribute their delicate, oniony flavour to fresh salads and raw vegetables. Chives should always be used fresh, as dried ones are virtually tasteless.

Coriander (also called cilantro): The serrated leaves of the coriander plant impart a distinctive fragrance and flavour that is both mildly sweet and bitter. Coriander leaves should be used fresh or added at the end of cooking if their flavour is to be appreciated fully.

Dill: A sprightly herb with feathery leaves, dill enhances cucumber and many other fresh vegetables, as well as fish and shellfish. When used in cooking, dill should be added towards the end of the process to preserve its delicate flavour. Both dill seeds and dill leaves can be